THE
ONLY GUIDE
TO A
WINNING
BOND
STRATEGY
YOU'LL EVER NEED

The Way Smart Money Preserves Wealth Today

◆

LARRY E. SWEDROE
AND
JOSEPH H. HEMPEN

◆

T·T

A TRUMAN TALLEY BOOK
ST. MARTIN'S PRESS ⚮ NEW YORK

www.stmartins.com

Library of Congress Cataloging-in-Publication Data

Swedroe, Larry E.
    The only guide to a winning bond strategy you'll ever need : the way smart money preserves wealth today / Larry E. Swedroe and Joseph H. Hempen.
        p. cm.
    "A Truman Talley book."
    ISBN 0-312-35363-4
    EAN 978-0-312-35363-6
    1. Bond. 2 Portfolio management. 3. Investments. I. Hempen, Joseph H. II. Title.

HG4651.S94 2005
332.63'23—dc22

                                                                                2005052949

First Edition: March 2006

10   9   8   7   6   5   4   3   2   1

To the employees of Buckingham Asset Management,
BAM Advisor Services LLC, and the advisors at the more than
one hundred independent fee-only Registered Investment
Advisor firms with whom we have strategic alliances.
Each and every one of them works diligently every day
to educate their clients on how markets really work and on
the benefits of a prudent, long-term investment strategy.

Contents

Contents

The inconvenience of going from rich to poor is greater than most people can tolerate. Staying rich requires an entirely different approach from getting rich. It might be said that one gets rich by working hard and taking big risks, and that one stays rich by limiting risk and not spending too much.

—*Investment Management*, edited by
Peter Bernstein and Aswath Damodaran

THE
ONLY GUIDE
TO A
WINNING
BOND
STRATEGY
YOU'LL EVER NEED

Introduction

Luck favors the prepared mind.   —Louis Pasteur

If you don't profit from your mistakes, someone else will.
       —Yale Hirsch

Despite its obvious importance to every individual, our education system almost totally ignores the field of finance and investments. Therefore, unless you earn an MBA in finance you probably never were taught how financial economists believe the markets work and how you can best make them work for you. The result is that most Americans, having taken a course in English literature in high school, have more knowledge about William Shakespeare than they do about investing. Without a basic understanding of financial markets and how they work there is simply no way for individuals to know how to make prudent investment decisions.

Most investors think they know how markets work. Unfortunately, the reality is quite different. As humorist Josh Billings noted: "It ain't what a man don't know as makes him a fool, but what he does know as ain't so." The result is that individuals are making investments without the basic knowledge required to understand the implications of their decisions. It is as if they took a trip to a place they have never been with neither a road map nor directions.

1

It is also unfortunate that many investors (and advisors) erroneously base their ideas and assumptions about fixed-income investing on their "knowledge" of equities. As you will learn, the two are completely different asset classes with different characteristics; even if the investor's thought process is correct on the equity side it may not be correct in the case of fixed income. The result is that the investor often makes suboptimal decisions.

While education can be expensive, ignorance is generally far more costly, especially in the investment world—a world filled with hungry wolves waiting to devour the innocent sheep. Fred Schwed relates the following tale in his book *"Where Are the Customers' Yachts? or a Good Hard Look at Wall Street."* An out-of-town visitor was being shown the wonders of the New York financial district. When his party arrived at the Battery, one of the guides indicated some handsome ships riding at anchor. He said, "Look, those are the bankers' and brokers' yachts." The naïve customer asked, "Where are the customers' yachts?" The yachts of the investment bankers and brokers are paid for by the ignorance of investors.

Benjamin Franklin said, "An investment in knowledge pays the best interest." Your investment in knowledge is the price of this book and the time you invest in reading it. The interest you receive will be the knowledge you need to be an informed fixed-income investor. Informed investors generally make far better investment decisions. And being an informed investor will help prevent you from being exploited by investment firms that take advantage of the lack of knowledge the general public has about fixed-income investing. The result is that it is more likely that you will be the one with the yacht, and not your broker.

When most investors begin their investment journey they focus on equity investing. Fixed-income investing is often an afterthought. This is unfortunate because for most individuals fixed-income investing plays an essential role in their overall investment strategy. Think of it this way, if your portfolio was a stew, fixed-income securities would be a main ingredient, like potatoes or carrots, not just a seasoning (e.g., salt, pepper) you add but might be able to leave out without adversely affecting the quality of the stew.

While there have been many books written on fixed-income investing, there have not been any that we are aware of that have met all of the following objectives:

- Educate you on the characteristics of all the types of fixed-income instruments available to investors, fully describing their risk and reward characteristics in plain and simple English.
- Address taxation and asset location issues (whether the asset is held in a taxable, tax deferred, or nontaxable account).
- Provide a practical road map to the winning strategy.
- Help you choose the most appropriate investment vehicles.
- Help you learn the best way to implement the winning strategy.
- Help you develop your own investment plan in the form of an investment policy statement (IPS).

The goals of this book are to meet all of these objectives and to convince you that while the world of fixed-income investing is a very complex one, the winning strategy is actually quite simple.

We begin with understanding that one of three motivations generally drive both individual and institutional investors to purchase fixed-income investments. The first is to provide liquidity to meet anticipated and unanticipated expenses. Any investments made for this reason should be highly liquid and should not be subject to any risk of loss of principal. Thus it belongs in such instruments as fully insured bank accounts, U.S. Treasury bills, and money-market mutual funds that invest in short-term instruments of the highest investment grade. This portion of your portfolio should really not even be considered an investment (which implies the taking of risk), but rather it is savings.

A second motivation to purchase fixed-income instruments is reduction of portfolio risk. Fixed-income assets allow investors to take equity risk while sleeping well and not panicking when the bear inevitably emerges from its hibernation. For investors in the accumulation stage of their investment life cycle (planning for retirement) this is generally the role that fixed income plays in a portfolio.

The third motivation for owning fixed-income assets is to create a steady stream of income or cash flow to meet ongoing expenses. This is usually the main role for fixed-income assets for those in the withdrawal stage of their investment life cycle. While the three reasons for owning fixed-income assets are not mutually exclusive, once individuals enter the withdrawal stage of their investment life cycle (usually upon retirement) this often becomes the primary motivation.

You will learn that whatever the motivation for investing in fixed-income assets, there are some simple guidelines to follow in order to give yourself the best chance of achieving your objectives. The rules of prudent fixed-income investing are:

- Purchase assets from the highest investment grades, avoiding instruments with a rating below AA.

- Purchase assets with a maturity that is short- to intermediate-term, avoiding long-term bonds.

- Avoid trying to outperform the market either by trying to guess the direction of interest rates (extending maturities when you believe rates will fall, and shortening them when you believe they will rise) or by trying to identify securities that are somehow mispriced by the market. There is simply no evidence that investors, either individuals or institutional, are *likely* to succeed in this effort. The winning strategy is to be a buy-and-hold investor.

- Avoid the purchase of what are called hybrid securities. These are instruments that have characteristics of both equities and fixed-income assets. Among the hybrid instruments we will discuss are convertible bonds, preferred stock, and high-yield bonds.

- Invest in only very low cost vehicles, avoiding whenever possible high cost funds, whether the high cost is in the form of high operating expenses or commissions (or loads). You will also learn that it is generally a very bad idea to buy individual bonds from a brokerage firm, a bank, or an investment bank (the markups, which are hidden, would shock you—and they are as legal as they are amoral).

We will begin our journey through the world of fixed-income investing by covering what might be called "bondspeak." In chapter 1 you will learn the "lingo" of the bond world. Unfortunately, without such knowledge you cannot make informed decisions. The second chapter is a detailed exploration of the risks of fixed-income investing. We then move on to discussing how bonds are bought and sold. Chapter 4 discusses how markets in general work. The knowledge gained will help lead you to the winning strategy. Chapters 5 through 9 cover the various taxable investments available to investors. We will discuss the pros and cons of each, and decide which instruments you should consider for purchase. Chapter 10 covers the world of municipal bond investing. Chapter 11 focuses on the development of a specific investment plan, an investment policy statement (IPS). It is designed to help you create your own unique plan. As you read through the book, use the glossary at the back for any technical terms you don't recognize.

Reading this book will not help to make you rich. It will, however, make you a better educated and, therefore, wiser investor. And, it may save you from turning a large fortune into a small one. We hope you enjoy the journey.

CHAPTER ONE

◆

Bondspeak

Good fortune is what happens when opportunity meets with planning. —Thomas Edison

While we search for the answers to the complex problem of how to live a longer life, there are simple solutions that can have a dramatic impact. For example, it would be hard to find better advice on living longer than do not smoke, drink alcohol in moderation, eat a balanced diet, get at least a half an hour of aerobic exercise three to four times a week, and buckle up before driving. The idea that complex problems can have simple solutions is not limited to the question of living a longer life. As Charles Ellis points out in *Winning the Loser's Game:* "Investment advice doesn't have to be complicated to be good." And this is certainly true, as you will learn, about the world of fixed-income investing.

The world of fixed-income investing was once a very simple one. It was also very conservative. When investors thought of fixed-income investing they thought of Treasury bonds, FDIC-insured savings accounts and certificates of deposits, and perhaps the bonds of blue chip corporations such as General Electric. Today, the world is a much more complex one. The research and marketing departments of investment firms regularly create new and highly complex debt instruments. Investors are now deluged with marketing campaigns from bond salesmen urging them to buy instruments such as MBS (mortgage-backed securities), IOs (interest-only bonds), POs (principal-only bonds), and inverse floaters (this one is too complex to describe in a short space).

The complexity of these debt instruments creates huge profit opportunities for Wall Street's sales forces. These complex securities are often sold to investors who generally don't understand the nature of the risks involved. And you can be sure that it is the rare salesman who fully explains the nature of the risks (most couldn't if they had to, as they are trained to sell, not to explain the risks of what they are selling). Thus investors end up taking risks that are not appropriate for their situation. They also incur large transaction costs that are often hidden in the form of markups and markdowns—a subject we will discuss in detail.

Unfortunately, there are investment firms that prey on retail investors who lack the knowledge to understand the risks involved and how these securities are valued by the market. One reason is that the prices for many fixed-income instruments, unlike those of stocks, cannot be found in the local newspaper, or even on the Internet. The lack of visibility in pricing allows for investor exploitation. Brian Reynolds, former institutional fixed-income portfolio manager at David J. Bradson & Company, commenting on this exploitation, stated: "When I went to buy bonds for myself, I was stunned at the difference between buying them as an institutional investor and as a retail investor."[1] Friend, and fellow investment author, William Bernstein put it this way: "The stockbroker services his clients in the same way that Bonnie and Clyde serviced banks."[2]

As was stated in the introduction, the first objective of this book is to provide you with the knowledge you need in order to make prudent investment decisions regarding fixed-income investments.

It is unlikely that Wall Street will ever provide you with this knowledge. In fact, the Wall Street Establishment does its best to follow W. C. Fields advice to "never smarten up a chump." Prudent investors never invest in any security unless they fully understand the nature of all of the risks. If you have ever bought (or been sold) a mortgage-backed security (e.g., a Ginnie Mae) the odds are pretty high that you bought a security the risks of which you did not fully understand. And those risks include paying too high a price.

As you will learn, it is not necessary to purchase complex instruments in order to have a good investment experience. Fortunately, the solutions to complex problems are often quite simple. In fact, the great likelihood is that you will do far better by simply hanging up the phone whenever someone tries to sell you one of these complex securities. The greatest likelihood is that they are products meant to be sold and not bought. A good question to consider asking the salesman is: "If these bonds are such good investments, why are you selling them to me instead of to your big institutional clients?" The answer should be obvious—either the institutions won't buy them, or the firm can make far greater profits from an exploitable public.

A Language of Its Own

Imagine you are an executive for a multinational corporation. You have been offered the position of general manager at your company's Paris office. Unfortunately, you don't speak French. Certainly one of the first things you would do would be to take an immersion course in the French language and culture. Doing so would enable you to more quickly gain an appreciation of your new environment, as well as prevent you from making some embarrassing, and potentially costly, mistakes.

Unfortunately, far too many investors take a trip to the land of bonds without knowing the language. Without such basic knowledge it is impossible to make informed decisions. In order to meet our objective of providing you with the knowledge needed to make prudent investment decisions we need to begin by exploring the language known as "bondspeak."

The world of fixed-income investing has its own language. This brief section defines the terms you need to understand in order to make prudent investment decisions. You will learn the difference between the primary (initial issue) and secondary (after initial offering) markets, and the wholesale (interdealer) and retail (individual investor) markets. You will also learn how bonds are bought from and sold to individual investors and the games broker-dealers play at your expense. After completing this relatively brief section you will have the knowledge required to understand the critical terminology of the world of bondspeak. We begin with some basic definitions.

A *bond* is a negotiable instrument (distinguishing it from a loan) evidencing a legal agreement to compensate the lender through periodic interest payments and the repayment of principal in full on a stipulated date. Bonds can either be secured or unsecured. An *unsecured* bond is one that is backed solely by a good-faith promise of the issuer. A *secured* bond is backed by a form of collateral. The collateral can be in the form of assets or revenue tied to a specific asset (e.g., tolls from a bridge or turnpike).

The document that spells out all of the terms of the agreement between the issuer and the holders is called the *indenture*. It identifies the issuer and their obligations, conditions of default, and actions that holders may take in the event of a default. It also identifies such features as calls and sinking fund requirements.

All of the important terms contained in the indenture are spelled out in the *prospectus*—the written statement that discloses the terms of a security's offering.

The *maturity* of a bond is the date upon which the repayment of principal is due. This differs specifically from "term-to-maturity" (or simply term) that reflects the number of years left until the maturity date. While most bond offerings have a single maturity, this is not the case for what is called a *serial bond* issue. Serial bonds are a series of individual bonds, with different maturities, from the same issuer. Investors do not have to purchase the entire series—they can purchase any of the individual securities. Typically, municipal bonds are serial bonds.

Although there are no specific rules regarding definitions, the general convention is to consider instruments that have a maturity of one year or less to be *short-term*. Instruments with a maturity of more than one and not more than ten years are considered to be *intermediate-term* bonds. And those whose maturity is greater than ten years are considered *long-term* bonds.

Treasuries are obligations that carry the *full faith and credit* of the U.S. government. The convention is that Treasury instruments with a maturity of up to six months are called Treasury *bills*. (The Treasury eliminated the one-year bill in 2001.) Treasury bills are issued at a discount to par (explanation to follow). The interest is paid in the form of the price rising toward par until maturity. Treasury instruments with a maturity of at least two years, but not greater than ten, are called *notes*. If the maturity is beyond ten years they are called *bonds*. Treasuries differ specifically from debt instruments of the government-sponsored enterprises (GSEs). The GSEs are the Federal Home Loan Banks (FLHBs), the Federal Farm Credit Banks, the Tennessee Valley Authority (TVA), the Federal National Mortgage Association (Fannie Mae), the Federal Home Loan Mortgage Corporation

(Freddie Mac), and a few others. While each was created by Congress to reduce borrowing costs for a specific sector of the economy, their obligations do not carry the full faith and credit of the U.S. government. In fact, Fannie Mae and Freddie Mac are publicly held corporations. In contrast, the securities of the Government National Mortgage Association (GNMA), because it is a government agency, do carry the full faith and credit of the U.S. government.

Par, Premium, and Discount

These terms refer to the price at which a bond is trading *relative* to its initial offering. Most bonds have a *face value* (the amount paid to the investor at maturity) of $1,000. They are also traded in blocks of a minimum of $1,000. *Par,* or 100 percent, is considered $1,000. A bond trading at 95 is trading below face value, and would be valued at $950 for each $1,000 of face value. A bond trading at 105 is trading above par and would be valued at $105,000 for each $100,000 of face value. A bond trading above par, or above 100, is called a *premium bond.* A bond will trade at a premium when the coupon (stated) yield is above the current market rate for a similar bond of the same remaining term-to-maturity. Consider a corporate bond with a ten-year maturity at issuance that has a coupon of 6 percent. Five years later the yield on a newly issued security from the same issuer, with the same credit rating, and a maturity of five years is being traded at a yield of 4 percent. Since the bond with the 6 percent coupon has the same credit risk and the same term risk it must trade at a higher price since it provides a higher coupon rate. The reverse would be true if in five years the current yield on a newly issued security with a maturity of five years is 8 percent. Since the new issue is yielding 8 percent and selling at 100, the instrument with a coupon rate of just 6 percent must trade below par. A bond trading below par, or 100, is called a *discount bond.*

From the above examples we can see that changes in the current price of a bond are inversely related to the change in interest rates—in general, rising (falling) interest rates result in lower (higher) bond prices.

There is an important point to discuss about premium and discount bonds. Many investors avoid premium bonds because they don't want to buy a bond that they perceive has a guaranteed loss built into the price—you pay above par yet receive only par at maturity. This is a major error. In fact, premium bonds offer advantages over discount bonds. First, the higher annual interest payments received offset the amortization of the premium paid. Second, because many investors (both retail and institutional) avoid premium bonds, they often provide a higher return than a comparable bond selling at par. Third, higher coupon bonds are *less* susceptible to the negative effect of rising interest rates on the price of a bond (we will discuss the reason behind this when we cover the subjects of interest rate risk and duration). Thus premium bonds sometimes offer both higher returns and less risk. Finally, for taxable bonds (not municipals), the IRS allows a one-time election to amortize (write down over time) the premium paid over the remaining life. The ability to deduct the amortized premium improves the after-tax return on the bond.

Investors, on the other hand, often prefer discount bonds, because they perceive an automatic profit—the difference between the discount price they paid and par that they will receive at maturity. However, the ultimate gain is offset by the below current market coupon received. In addition, there is a potential negative to purchasing discount bonds in a taxable account—the discount may be treated as a gain for tax purposes and thus taxable at maturity. This will be the case unless when amortized over the remaining life the discount is less than 0.25 percent per annum. Finally, another negative of discount bonds is that bonds with lower coupons are subject to greater interest rate risk—they are *more* susceptible to the negative effect of rising interest rates on the price of a bond.

Calls and Puts

Calls

The term *call* is important to understand as its presence greatly impacts the risks and *potential* rewards of owning a bond. The failure to understand the risks of owning a bond with a call feature creates the potential for large losses and investors being abused by amoral (though not illegal) practices of broker-dealers (a subject we will cover shortly). Most municipal and agency bonds, as well as some corporate bonds, have a feature that gives the issuer the right, but not the obligation, to prepay the principal (prior to maturity) on a specific date or dates. This feature, known as a call, creates significant risk to investors, for which they do receive a higher coupon (yield) as compensation. The higher yield creates the potential for greater returns but also, depending on the price paid for the bond, the potential for losses. The risk results from the fact that the issuer will only call the bond if interest rates have fallen significantly since the time of issuance (rates need to have fallen sufficiently to overcome the cost of a new issue to replace the original one). For example, investors who originally bought a bond yielding 5 percent will have their bond called at a time when the current yield might be just 3 percent. Thus investors will not have earned 5 percent for the full term of the original bond. When the issuer calls the bond, the principal will be returned. The investor must reinvest the proceeds at the now lower market rate of 3 percent. Another negative feature of a callable bond is that it limits the potential for a bond to appreciate in price if interest rates fall.

A related term is the *period of call protection.* This is a period during which the issuer cannot call the bond.

There is a specific type of bond that has an implied call feature. *Mortgage-backed securities* (MBS), sometimes called *mortgage pass-through certificates,* are debt instruments for which an undivided interest in a pool of mortgages serves as the underlying asset (collateral) for the security. Because borrowers have the right to prepay their mortgage at any time, MBS have an implied call feature. Thus, while MBS have a known maturity, investors can only estimate the timing of the receipt of principal payments. Because of this implied call feature, the estimated maturity is inversely related to interest rates—as interest rates fall (rise), the estimated term of the principal payments shortens (lengthens).

There is another feature that is in the *indenture* (terms of agreement) of some bonds that is related to the call feature in how it can impact the risks and rewards of bond ownership. This feature is known as a *sinking fund.*

A Sinking Fund

A sinking fund is a provision in the indenture of a bond that requires the issuer to retire, using a prearranged schedule, a certain amount of the debt each year. Sinking funds are most common for longer-term municipal bond issues. The issuer will either purchase the bonds in the open market if the price is below par (100), or call the bonds at the prearranged price (typically par). The determination as to which specific bonds are to be called is usually done by a lottery.

There are some advantages to a sinking fund provision. First, it improves the credit quality of the issue over time as less debt is outstanding. A second reason for the lower yield is that the sinking fund provision shortens the average maturity of the bond (while not always the case, shorter maturities typically have lower yields—the yield curve is positively sloped).

There are also negatives of a sinking fund feature. First, if interest rates have fallen since issuance and your bond is chosen to be redeemed by the lottery drawing, then you lose the now above market yield, having to replace it with a lower yielding instrument. Second, some bonds with sinking funds have what is called an optional acceleration feature, allowing them to retire more of the debt than scheduled. Of course the issuer will only exercise the option if it is to their advantage to do so, meaning that it is not in the investor's interest. This acceleration feature can even supersede the call protection period.

Puts

A *put* gives the investor the right, but not the obligation, to redeem the security on a specific date that is prior to maturity. A put is an attractive feature for investors as it offers protection against rising interest rates. A put is thus a form of insurance, for which investors are willing to pay a premium. That premium comes in the form of a lower interest rate.

Zero-Coupon Bond

A zero-coupon bond is a bond that receives no interest payments. It is sold at a discount to par and then accretes (gradually increases) in value over time the imputed (or phantom) interest. Unlike coupon bonds, zero-coupon bonds have no reinvestment risk (to be discussed shortly) because no interest is actually paid out (the "interest" does not have to be reinvested—the reinvestment in effect occurs automatically).

We will now move on to terms that are specifically related to the yield of a bond.

Terms Related to Yield

Yield can be thought of as the price of risk. The risk can be in the form of interest rate risk, credit risk, or liquidity risk. There are many terms related to yield and it is imperative for investors to thoroughly understand each of them. We begin with the term *coupon yield*. The coupon yield is the stated fixed (or floating) percentage of the face amount (principal) paid as interest each year until maturity. This is specifically in contrast to the *current yield*—the percentage income you receive in relation to the current price (not the face value). Current yield also differs from *yield-to-maturity* (YTM).

The yield-to-maturity is a return calculation that takes into account not only the interest payments, but also the change in price of the bond from the time of purchase until maturity. A more precise definition for yield-to-maturity would be the *discount rate,* when applied to all cash flows, that results in the present value of the bond equal to the price paid. Yield-to-maturity is a far superior, though not perfect, measure of return than current yield or coupon yield. The primary benefit of using yield-to-maturity is that it allows investors to compare securities with different coupons and prices in a more apples-to-apples manner.

It is crucial to understand that for bonds with call features, yield-to-maturity is not the only measure that should be used. Investors need to also consider measures known as "yield-to-call" and "yield-to-worst." The *yield-to-call* is a return calculation that treats the call date as the maturity date. An example will illustrate the point. A bond is issued in 2000 with a 6 percent coupon with a maturity of 2020. However, the indenture allows the bond to be called in 2010 at par. By 2005 interest rates have fallen substantially so that the issuer could replace their old obligation with new debt with the same maturity at a rate of just 4 percent. If rates remain unchanged the issuer will then call the bond in 2010. Thus the expected maturity is no longer 2020 (remaining term of fifteen years), but is instead 2010 (remaining term of just five years.) Because the coupon of 6 percent is above the current market rate, the bond will trade above par. Let's assume that the bond is trading at 112. The yield-to-maturity must be less than 6 percent because the investor is paying 112 and will only receive 100 at maturity. The twelve-point premium must be amortized over the remaining life (fifteen years) to determine the yield-to-maturity. Once the premium is considered, the yield-to-maturity falls to about 4.7 percent. However, the call date is just five years away. If the bond were to be called in 2010 the ten-point premium the investor paid will have to be amortized over just five years, instead of fifteen. The result is that the yield-to-call will be much lower—about 3.5 percent. The market will treat the bond as if it has just five years left to maturity.

If a bond involves one or more call dates, then a calculation must be made for what is called *yield-to-worst*. Yield-to-worst is a return calculation that considers the yield-to-call for every possible call date. The call date with the lowest yield-to-call is the one with the yield-to-worst. Yield-to-worst is especially important when purchasing a bond with a sinking fund as you cannot be sure of the maturity.

The next term we need to discuss is generally used in reference to tax-exempt bonds. Since income from most municipal bonds is exempt from federal taxes (and generally from state and local taxes when buying bonds from one's home state) a mechanism is needed to provide a comparison of yields on a pretax basis. (Interest on bonds issued by the U.S. territories of Puerto Rico, the Virgin Islands, Guam, American Samoa, and the Northern Mariana Islands is also exempt from federal, state, and local income taxes.)

The *tax equivalent yield* (TEY) tells an investor the rate of return that would have to be earned on a taxable bond in order for the taxable bond to provide the same after-tax rate of return. The formula is relatively simple and provides a good approximation (due to differences in how states treat municipal bond interest) of the TEY. The tax equivalent yield is equal to the yield on the municipal bond divided by 100 percent minus the applicable tax bracket.

$$TEY = Y / (100\% - \text{effective federal and state tax rate})$$

Keep in mind that interest on U.S. government obligations is exempt from state and local taxes, but interest on other taxable bonds (i.e., corporate bonds) is not. Thus if the investor's residence is one in which there is a state income tax, the investor would require different yields from a Treasury bond and a corporate bond of the same maturity—the corporate yield would have to be higher. This example explains why part of the higher yield investors require on corporate bonds over Treasury bonds is related to the difference in tax treatment. The other reasons for the higher required return are credit risk and liquidity risk.

There is another yield term that is specifically related to the yield on fixed-income mutual funds. The *SEC yield* is a standard yield calculation that is required to be used by mutual funds. Its purpose is to allow investors to make accurate comparisons between mutual funds. It considers the return over the prior thirty days, changes in the price of bonds as they move toward par over the period, and the fund's expenses. Note that one limitation of the SEC yield is that it is not useful when considering funds that buy securities denominated in foreign currencies and simultaneously hedge the currency risk. The reason is that the SEC doesn't consider the hedge, only the interest, in the calculation. In addition, it can be a very misleading measure of the return the investor will earn over time, as it measures only the yield over the past thirty days. Mutual funds know that investors, because they do not fully understand the risks of fixed-income investing, are often attracted solely by a measure such as the SEC yield (thinking the higher the better). A fund can drive up the SEC yield by purchasing very high coupon bonds. However, if those bonds are likely to be called, the SEC yield will prove very misleading. The fund could also drive up the yield by purchasing riskier credits.

We now move on to what is called the *yield curve*—a curve that graphically depicts the yields of bonds of the same credit quality but different maturities. The yield is depicted on the vertical axis and the maturity on the horizontal. The yield curve depicts what is called the *term structure of interest rates*. The most commonly referenced yield curve is the one reflecting the term structure of U.S. Treasury instruments. Yield curves can be constructed for other instruments such as municipal bonds and corporate bonds. Curves can also be constructed for more narrowly defined sectors of the market. For example, there is a different curve for AAA-rated and BBB-rated corporate bonds.

Normally the yield curve is upward (positively) sloping—the longer the maturity, the higher the interest rate demanded by investors. This reflects the demand for a risk premium—the longer the maturity of a bond, the greater it is subject to price risk, and, therefore, the higher the return required to bear that risk. However, there have been periods of both flat yield curves (rates are similar across the curve, from short to long) and inverted (negatively sloping) curves (when short-term rates are higher than long-term rates). An inverted curve generally occurs when the Federal Reserve Bank engages in a severe tightening of the money supply in order to fight inflation. This drives short-term interest rates up sharply. However, investors expect that the sharp rise in short-term rates will lead to a slowing down of both inflation and the economy. Thus they anticipate that interest rates will eventually fall. The result is that long-term rates are lower than short-term rates.

There is one more critical point we need to cover in relation to the yield curve. The riskier the investment, the steeper the yield curve is likely to be because credit risk is positively correlated with maturity (the longer the maturity, the greater the credit risk). For example the spread (the difference in yields) between one and thirty-year U.S. Treasuries will be less than the spread between one- and thirty-year AAA-rated corporate bonds, which will in turn be less than the spread between one- and thirty-year BBB-rated bonds.

Now that you have an understanding of the basic terms related to fixed-income investing we can move on to the risks of investing in debt securities.

CHAPTER TWO

◆

The Risks of Fixed-Income Investing

The market acts as a big insurance company. It transfers risk from those that want to avoid it, to those that are willing to accept it, assuming they receive an insurance, or risk, premium. —William Sharpe, Nobel Prize winner.

The word "crisis" in Chinese is composed of two characters. The first is the symbol of danger, the second the symbol of opportunity. —Unknown

One of the fundamental principles of finance is the positive relationship between risk and *expected* reward. The concept is easy to grasp and can be summed up in the adage "Nothing ventured, nothing gained." While the concept is simple, the reality for fixed-income investors is much more complex. The reason is that investors in fixed-income securities can incur as many as eight different types of risks—each with its own implications that should be thoroughly understood. The eight types of risks are interest rate risk, credit risk, reinvestment risk, inflation risk, event risk, tax risk, liquidity risk, and agency risk. This chapter provides a thorough explanation of each of the risks and their implications for investment policy.

Knowledge of the risks involved allows for the design of safer portfolios. For example, shipbuilders know that, in most cases, the seas are relatively safe. However, they also know that typhoons and hurricanes happen. Therefore, they design their ships not just for the 95 percent of the sailing days when the weather is clement, but also for the other 5 percent, when storms blow and their skill is tested.[1] What follows is the equivalent of weather warnings to mariners. Hopefully, you will avoid the fate of the mariners who failed to heed weather warnings.

Interest Rate Risk

Interest rate risk (also known as price risk) refers to the risk that the price of a security will fall due to an increase in interest rates. A basic concept is that interest rate risk is positively correlated with maturity—the longer the maturity of the instrument, the greater the interest rate risk. This is because, all else being equal, the longer the maturity of a bond, the greater will be the percentage change in price for a given change in interest rates. Investors need to understand, however, that the relationship between maturity and price risk is not linear. Again, all else being equal, the lower (higher) the coupon interest rate, the greater (smaller) will be the change in price for a given change in interest rates. Also note, again all else being equal, that for a given change in interest rates callable bonds will change less in price than noncallable bonds. A good example of this occurs when a callable bond is trading above par (because interest rates have fallen since issuance). If interest rates fall farther, the callable bond will not be very sensitive to the fall in rates because of the risk that the right to call (redeem) the bond will be exercised. In fact, its price might not rise at all, and it might actually fall. This is typically what happens to mortgage-backed bonds that are already trading at a significant premium since the risk of prepayment increases (the price actually falls despite the fall in interest rates). The reason the price falls is that prepayments on the mortgages backing the security will rise and the premium paid will have to be amortized over a shorter period.

Interest rate risk is best measured using a concept known as *duration.* Duration is a complex concept that even has different forms (there is what is known as Macaulay duration, there is also modified duration, and even option-adjusted duration). It is beyond the scope of this book to delve into these differences. In simple terms, however, you can think of duration as the percentage change in the price of a bond that can be expected given a percentage change in the yield on that bond. This is what is known as modified duration. For example, if interest rates rise (fall) 1 percent, a bond with a duration of one will fall (rise) in price by about 1 percent, and a bond with a duration of seven will fall (rise) by about 7 percent. In more precise mathematical terms duration is the sum of the time-weighted discounted cash flows received divided by the price paid. This is what is known as Macaulay duration.

An example will help explain the concept of duration. Take two bonds, each with a maturity of twenty years. Bond X, a AAA-rated bond, carries a coupon of 5 percent and Bond Y, a BBB-rated bond carries a coupon of 10 percent. Each bond trades at par, or 100. The series of payments received by the holder of Bond X will be $5 in years one through nineteen and $105 in year twenty. Bond Y holders will receive $10 in year one through nineteen and $110 in year twenty. The holders of Bond Y are receiving cash flow at a faster pace. In year one Bond X holders receive just 5 percent of the amount invested, while Bond Y holders receive 10 percent. By year ten holders of Bond X have received just 50 percent of their principal back, while holders of Bond Y have received 100 percent (without considering the interest on reinvested interest payments) Think of it this way, Bond Y holders have their investment (principal) outstanding on average for a shorter time. Thus Bond Y should be less sensitive to a given change in interest rates. Specifically, the duration of these two bonds is about 11 for Bond Y with the 10 percent coupon, and closer to 13 for Bond X with the 5 percent coupon. The longer duration of Bond X indicates a greater sensitivity of price to any given change in interest rates. Thus you can see that while Bond X has less credit risk, it has greater interest rate risk. And the reverse is true for Bond Y—it has greater credit risk but less interest rate risk.

In the simplest terms possible one can think of duration as the average amount of time that the principal is outstanding discounted at the current market yield for that security. And all else being equal, the lower (higher) the coupon, the longer (shorter) the duration. Thus bonds with high coupons have less price risk than bonds with low coupons. Zero-coupon bonds, which pay no interest until maturity, have the longest duration—their duration is the same as their term-to-maturity—and thus the greatest price risk. The concept of duration allows investors to compare the price risk of bonds that have different maturities, call dates, and coupon rates. Note that duration has its limits. For example, it only works well for relatively small changes in interest rates.

Credit Risk

Credit risk refers to the potential for the issuer of the instrument to default, failing to pay interest or principal or both. Just as you can judge the safety of many products by referring to their safety ratings from independent sources such as *Consumer Reports,* the credit risk of a particular security can be gauged by examining the ratings given by the commercial rating agencies. The largest of these companies are Standard & Poor's, Moody's, Duff & Phelps, and Fitch.

The credit rating of the instrument is not always a good indicator of the credit risk of the issuer. The reason is that the rating of a particular security reflects its own unique credit characteristics. Thus it is possible that a single issuer can have bonds that trade with different credit ratings. Of course, the market will require that bonds with lower credit ratings provide greater yields as compensation for their greater risk. Therefore, investors should not assume that the bond that carries the higher yield is the superior investment when comparing two bonds from the same issuer. What it does mean is that it is a riskier investment. For example, a rating may be enhanced by the use of collateral or the purchase of credit insurance. Therefore, it would carry a higher credit rating than a bond without such an enhancement, and the market would price that bond with a lower yield than if there was no enhancement. Thus it is vital that investors check the rating of the

Credit Ratings of Standard & Poor's and Moody's

Standard & Poor's	Moody's	Moody's Description of Risk
AAA	Aaa	Almost riskless, just below U.S. Treasury obligations. Future changes *unlikely* to impair debt rating.
AA	Aa	High quality. Future changes *may* impair rating.
A	A	Good quality. *Susceptible* to impairment of rating.
BBB	Baa	Medium quality; lowest investment grade. Have *some speculative characteristics*.
BB	Ba	*Speculative*; noninvestment grade
B, CCC, CC	B, Caa	Very speculative
C	Ca	Extremely speculative
D	C	Default

specific issue. It is also important to understand that the longer the maturity, the greater the credit risk. The table above provides the credit ratings of the two largest agencies, along with a brief explanation.

There is an important point about the above ratings of which most investors are unaware, and would probably be surprised to learn—not all AAA bonds are created equal. Based on the historical evidence, municipal bonds with a AAA rating have a lower risk of default than do similarly rated corporate bonds. And the same would be true of any two municipal and corporate bonds with the same rating—the municipal bond is less risky from a credit perspective. In fact, a Moody's study found that when compared by individual rating category, municipal bonds are about ten times less likely to default than similarly rated corporate debt.[2] The differential is even more dramatic when we consider only investment-grade bonds.

A. G. Edwards found that over the thirty years ending in 2004 overall default rates for investment-grade corporate bonds were almost *ninety* times higher than investment-grade municipal bonds. In fact, the distinction is so great that Moody's states: "If municipalities were rated on the corporate scale, Moody's would likely assign Aaa ratings to the vast majority of general obligation debt issued by fiscally sound, large municipal issuers." Moody's goes on to note that "nearly all performing municipal general obligation and essential service revenue bonds would be rated Aa3 or higher on the corporate rating scale." Similarly, Moody's views a Baa3 municipal general obligation bond as being at least as creditworthy as an Aa3 corporate bond, and so on down the credit chain. Historical default rates bear this out—the overall default rate for investment-grade municipal bonds is approximately one-half the default rate for Triple-A corporate bonds.[3]

As further evidence of the safety of investment-grade municipal bonds, over the period 1970–2000 only eighteen municipal bonds rated investment grade by Moody's defaulted. And the average one-year default rate was just 0.01 percent. This compares to a one-year default rate of 1.3 percent on similarly rated corporate bonds.[4]

Note, however, that if a municipal bond falls below the investment-grade category the risk of default increases *sixty times*. The comparable increase for corporate bonds is fourteen times. Clearly there is a difference in credit risk between municipal and corporate bonds and how rating differentials indicate differences in credit risk.[5] One conclusion we can draw is that conservative investors should think carefully about investing in any instrument that is below investment grade.

There is another important point of which investors in municipal bonds should be aware. There are certain sectors of the municipal bond market that have historically experienced higher rates of default. And, as was explained above, due to the greater risk of default the market will require higher yields as compensation for the greater risk. Three such sectors are health care, multi-family housing, and industrial development bonds. Recent research from Fitch, however, found that within the health care sector it is crucial to differentiate among subsectors. Fitch found that hospital-related bonds had much lower default rates than those related to nursing homes and long-term health care facilities. For hospitals the default rate was only 0.63 percent as compared to a default rate of over 17 percent for nonhospitals. Clearly investors need to differentiate among these subsectors.[6]

The bottom line is that for investors considering municipal bonds, and whose main objective is the safety of principal for their taxable fixed-income investments, the prudent strategy is to stick with investment-grade munis and avoid those sectors that have exhibited greater default risk.

In addition to the aforementioned eight risks, there are two other risks investors must understand: systematic and unsystematic risk. When investors become familiar with these two types of risk, they will better understand how their portfolio works because the relationship between systematic/unsystematic risk, and expected return applies to all securities (whether fixed income or equities).

Systematic versus Unsystematic Risk

The Talmud is considered the authoritative record of rabbinic discussions on Jewish law, ethics, and customs. In addition, it is the basis for all later codes of Jewish law. It is thousands of years old. It is clear that even the rabbinical sages who wrote the Talmud understood the benefits of diversification. The Talmud admonishes: "Let every man divide his money into three parts, and invest a third in land, a third in business, and a third let him keep in reserve." Even Shakespeare, in *The Merchant of Venice,* showed that he understood the importance of diversification: "My ventures are not in one bottom [ship] trusted, nor to one place, nor is my whole estate upon the fortune of this present year. Therefore, my merchandise makes me not sad."

One of the basic principles of prudent investing is that the diversification of risk is essential with both stocks and bonds. However, the diversification issue is significantly different for bonds than it is for stocks. In order to understand this critical difference, we need to understand the difference between what is called *systematic* and *unsystematic* risk.

A risk that is systematic is one that cannot be diversified away. For example, a farmer cannot diversify away the risk that a flood, drought, insects, plague, or other adverse event could destroy all of his crops. He can, however, diversify the risk of the price he receives being below expectation. Unsystematic risk is risk that can be diversified away. For example, a farmer would be taking unsystematic risk if he planted only soybeans. Instead, he might also plant corn, wheat, and sorghum. If the Brazilian soybean crop were to be so large that it would drive down the price of soybeans, the farmer might still be able to receive sufficiently high prices for his other crops to prevent serious problems. By diversifying what he plants, he avoids the problem of trusting his entire fortune to a single crop—he gains protection against a blight that might impact one crop but not another.

Investors must be rewarded for taking systematic risk or they would not take it. That reward is in the form of a risk premium, a higher *expected* return than could be earned by investing in a less risky instrument. For example, investors in stocks can logically *expect* to earn a premium over the return on Treasury bills since they take more risk. Since 1926 that risk premium has been about 7 percent per annum. Of course, that premium is not earned every year, or there would be no risk (and no risk premium). If some investors had forgotten that point, the bear market of 2000–02 provided a painful reminder. The market, however, does not reward investors for risks they can avoid through diversification. The following examples will help illustrate these points.

Let's assume an investor owns only shares of Merck, a pharmaceutical company. That is risk that can be easily diversified away; thus it is unsystematic risk. For example, the investor could reduce the single stock risk by also purchasing shares of Johnson & Johnson (J&J). In addition to both being pharmaceutical companies, they are both large growth stocks. Without going beyond the scope of this book, it is essential to understand that despite what many investors believe, the academic evidence is that two large growth stocks (even if they are from different industries) have the same expected return (assuming their book-to-market [or price-to-earnings] ratio and market capitalization are similar).

Since Merck and J&J have the same expected return, we can re-duce risk by diversifying—owning both instead of trying to guess which will be the better performer.

Taking the example one step further, we could again reduce risk by purchasing shares in a sector fund that owns shares of all of the pharmaceutical companies. Owning an entire sector is less risky than owning just a single stock, or a few stocks. However, our investor is still left with unsystematic risk because there is still risk that can be diversified away—the risk of that single sec-tor or industry. This risk can be diversified away by owning an S&P 500 Index fund.

Summing up, in simple terms, investors should expect to re-ceive the same return whether they invest in any of the three al-ternatives presented—the single stock, the sector fund, or an S&P 500 Index fund. In each case the investor should expect to be re-warded *only* for taking the risk of owning equities. The risk of owning the single stock, or the sector fund, does not provide in-vestors with any higher expected return.

While the risk of owning stocks in general explains a large per-centage of the returns of any individual company, a very signifi-cant portion of the returns of a single stock result from the unique characteristics (risks) of that particular stock. Thus a prudent in-vestor should draw the conclusion that diversification is the win-ning strategy. The reason is that diversification *reduces the risk* of investing in equities *without reducing expected returns*. The point is so important that it is worth repeating. Diversification is the only free lunch in investing because through diversification in-vestors reduce risk without lowering their expected return.

The most efficient way to diversify with stocks is to own a low-cost and tax-efficient mutual fund, or what is called an exchange-traded fund (ETF). An ETF is similar to a closed-end mutual fund in that it trades like a stock—it can be bought and sold during the day. In addition, it does not necessarily trade at its net asset value (NAV)—although professional arbitrageurs basically ensure that the price does not vary much from its NAV. Open-end mutual funds can only be bought and sold at the end of the day, and they trade at their NAV. (Chapter 11 discusses the pros and cons of ETFs, mutual funds, and individual securities.)

There is an important difference between stocks and bonds that impacts the relative importance of diversification. Understanding the difference helps us formulate the winning strategy. With equity investing, broad diversification is extremely important. We will now determine why diversification is significantly less important in fixed-income investing.

Bonds: Birds of a Feather Flock Together

We have learned that we can substantially reduce the risks of equity investing through diversification because we can diversify away the unsystematic risk that plays a large role in equity returns. One of the major differences between fixed-income and equity investing is that almost all of the return from a fixed-income investment (at least for high-credit-quality bonds) is determined by risk that cannot be diversified away—it is systematic risk. That risk is the result of price changes caused by changes in interest rates. (This risk can be diversified by holding bonds of various maturities; specifically a laddered portfolio, which we will discuss in chapter 11.) Very little of the returns of highly rated investment-grade bonds is determined by unsystematic risk—characteristics that are unique to the issuer of the security. For example, for the period 1926–2003 the correlation of returns of long-term government bonds and long-term corporate bonds was a very high 0.934

(1.0 would be perfect correlation). The conclusion we draw from the data is that most of the return on corporate bonds is explained by the return on government bonds. Since government bonds have no credit risk, the only thing explaining their return is interest rates. Thus we can conclude that almost all of the returns of high-credit-quality fixed-income instruments are derived from interest rate risk, which cannot be diversified away—it is systematic risk.

The implication is that while it is critical to diversify the risks of equity investing (to minimize or eliminate the unsystematic risk), because most of the returns of high-credit-quality fixed-income securities comes from interest rate risk, the benefits of, and thus the need for, diversification are substantially reduced. With U.S. government debt the need for diversification of *credit* risk is nonexistent—100 percent of the risk is systematic risk (in this case interest rate risk) that cannot be diversified away.

Think of it this way, bonds of the highest investment grades are commodities—bonds of the same maturity and same high credit quality are good substitutes for each other (unlike the stocks of Merck and J&J which are not as good substitutes for each other). The result is that while it would not be prudent to build an equity portfolio by selecting a small sample of stocks, prudent diversification of credit risk can be accomplished with a relatively small sample of high-credit quality bonds (ten to perhaps twenty-five).

The higher the credit quality, the more confident you can be that a relatively small sample will produce very similar returns to that produced by the entire population of similarly rated bonds of the same maturity—and the less significant diversification becomes. (We will discuss later the implication this has on the decision to own individual bonds or to purchase mutual funds.) Conversely, the lower the credit quality, the more significant the need for diversification of fixed-income assets becomes. For example, two high-yield bonds are not good substitutes for one another—they are far less likely to provide similar returns than two AAA-rated bonds. Thus if an investor sought the higher expected returns that high-yield bonds provide she should do so through a mutual fund and not through the purchase of individual bonds. The reason is that it would be very hard for her to sufficiently diversify a portfolio of high-yield bonds. Thus the prudent course would be to own a mutual fund that owned the bonds of many (perhaps one hundred or more) different companies. Of course she has to pay for that benefit in the form of the expenses of a fund. Thus the potential for higher yield is somewhat offset by the expenses of operating the fund (as well as the incremental credit risk).

In terms of the diversification of credit risk there are some additional insights we need to explore. First, while the number of holdings is important, diversification is not determined solely by the number of different issuers in the portfolio. For example, if you held ten securities and one of the ten represented 90 percent of the dollar holdings, then the portfolio would not be well diversified. Second, if most of the holdings are from issuers in the same sector (e.g., hospitals, airlines, hotels) then the portfolio would not be well diversified. It would be as if an investor owned one hundred different stocks but all of them were technology stocks. The issue is one of identifying whether the risks of the various issuers defaulting are highly correlated (that is, as the risk of default increases for one, it increases for the others). Thus credit risk needs to be diversified not only from the perspective of the issuer, but also from the perspective of sector or industry concentration, geographic concentration, and economic risk concentration.

Reinvestment Risk

Reinvestment risk is the risk that future interest and principal payments when received and reinvested may earn less than current rates. In terms of the interest payments, the reinvestment risk increases as you extend maturity. (The interest rates you will earn when reinvesting the interest payments as they are received may be lower than interest rates were when the bond was purchased.) The reason is that the longer the maturity, the greater the potential for a fall in interest rates. However, in terms of the principal payment, the shorter the maturity, the greater the reinvestment risk. Long-term bonds lock in the rate of interest earned on the principal. With short-term bonds the principal must be rolled over frequently. Thus the rate of interest that will be earned over a long period of time is at risk. A call feature increases reinvestment risk. Mortgage-backed securities (MBS), because of their implied call feature, have a high degree of reinvestment risk. On the other hand, zero-coupon bonds have no reinvestment risk (unless the issue is callable).

Inflation Risk

Unless a bond is an inflation-protected security (i.e., a TIPS) it earns a nominal interest rate, unadjusted for inflation. Inflation erodes the real return earned by investors, the only kind of return that matters. The longer the maturity of an instrument, the greater the inflation risk incurred. The reason is that nominal interest rates incorporate the market's expectation of future inflation—the longer the horizon, the greater the risk that actual inflation will exceed that expectation.

Event Risk

Event risk is the risk that something unexpected will occur that will impact the ability of the issuer to repay. It might be an act of nature (e.g., a hurricane), an environmental issue (e.g., oil spill, asbestos-related problem), an act of terrorism, or other unantici-pated misfortunes. Corporate bonds also have a type of event risk that is unique to them. The following is an example of this very specific type of event risk. An investor purchases an AA-rated corporate bond. A BBB-rated company later acquires the issuer. The acquiring company assumes the obligations of the issuer and thus the investor is left holding a BBB-rated bond instead of an AA-rated one. There are other ways that the risk of a corporate bond can change due to a change in the capital structure. For ex-ample, a firm could decide to engage in a leveraged buyout of its stock and take the firm private. The increase in debt incurred to buy out the equity almost certainly will lower the credit rating, and quite possibly lower it dramatically. Another example would be if a firm made an acquisition that required large amounts of debt. The potential for event risk negatively impacting corporate bonds is one reason that they have experienced much higher de-fault rates than similarly rated municipal bonds. Thus it is neces-sary for investors to understand that a AAA rating does not indicate the same degree of safety with a corporate bond as it does with a similarly rated municipal bond. The bottom line on event risk is that it is credit risk.

Tax Risk

For some securities there is the risk that changes in the tax law can negatively impact the price of a bond. That is why this type of risk is also known as regulatory risk. For example, a lowering (or elim-ination) of the federal or state income tax rate would negatively impact the demand for municipal bonds relative to taxable instru-ments. Or there could be a change in the tax treatment of unrelated items, such as qualified dividends, that could increase the compe-tition from taxable instruments, again negatively impacting the price of municipals. In addition, over the years there have been discussions about removing the federal tax exemption for municipal bonds. Clearly, such an action would negatively impact their price. The longer the time frame, the greater is the risk that such legislation will be passed.

Liquidity Risk

Liquidity refers to the ease and cost related to trading a security at its true value. A security that is highly liquid is one for which the spread between the bid and the offer is very small, and for which large amounts can be bought and sold without the buyer or seller incurring significant market impact costs (i.e., moving the market price against themselves). The most liquid instruments are those issued by the U.S. Treasury. The less liquid the market for a security, the greater will be the risk premium (higher yield) demanded by investors. Investors should note the following: The riskier the credit, the more illiquid the security. The more actively traded a security, the lesser the liquidity risk.

The world of art presents a great example of how liquidity, or the lack of it, impacts trading costs.

Artwork is an asset that is highly illiquid. Artwork (and other collectables) is traded on a far less frequent basis than most securities. The lack of frequent trading creates risk for buyers. The result of the lack of liquidity is that the bid-offer spread is typically very wide. A spread of 15 to 20 percent is perhaps typical. Yet spreads can be much wider. And at times there may be no bid at all, or at least no bid that a willing seller would accept. An example from the bond world is the yield spread between what are called *on-the-run* Treasury securities and what are called *off-the-run* Treasuries.

The Treasury market is the most liquid market in the world.

And while all Treasury securities are relatively liquid, not all Treasuries have the same degree of liquidity. The most actively traded, and thus the most liquid (with the lowest trading costs), Treasury securities are the newly issued ones. Thus newly issued securities are the ones most favored by traders. When the Treasury issues a new ten-year bond the new bond replaces the prior ten-year bond as the one favored by traders. The newly issued ten-year bond is called the on-the-run security, while the one it replaced is called the off-the-run security. Because the off-the-run security is now less liquid, the market prices it at a discount (higher yield) to the on-the-run security. Thus, even though the off-the-run security has a shorter maturity it will typically trade at a discount to the otherwise very similar on-the-run security. It is worth noting that buy-and-hold investors who are not as concerned about liquidity as traders should prefer buying the off-the-run securities (assuming they can avoid large dealer markups) in order to earn the higher yield. Since they don't care as much about liquidity (or at least believe that there is little risk of having to sell prior to maturity), the liquidity premium, while not being a "free lunch" (if there is any risk of having to sell prior to maturity there is no "free lunch"), might be considered a "free stop at the dessert tray." This goes against the conventional wisdom that the best way to buy bonds is in the primary market (initial offering) and not in the secondary market. The same consideration applies to municipals, where the secondary market for most securities is highly illiquid.

Agency Risk

There is a type of risk that only applies to investors in funds, not individual securities. There is always some risk that the manager of a fund will take greater risk than the investor anticipated. For example, in 2002 Vanguard's Total Bond Index Fund (VBMFX) made a large bet by overweighting bonds of issuers from the telecommunications sector. When those bonds performed poorly, the fund underperformed its benchmark index by 2 percent. This is a particularly good example, because of Vanguard's reputation as a conservative and well-run mutual fund company.

There is also the risk of fraud. Such risks are known as agency risks. Losses that occur through agency risk are often devastating, in some cases leading to a total loss of principal.

Having completed our survey of the various risks investors in fixed-income securities face, we now move on to exploring the various segments that make up the bond market. We will also discuss how bonds are bought and sold in each of them.

CHAPTER THREE

◆

The Buying and Selling of Individual Bonds

It may be said that the long-term goal of investing is to multiply the eggs in our baskets. Yet too many investors focus on producing more eggs (getting high returns) while paying little attention to the fox (costs) that perpetually robs the henhouse. If you ignore the fox, soon there will be nothing left to produce more eggs.

—Scott West and Mitch Anthony,
Storyselling for Financial Advisors

John Bogle, founder and former chairman of the Vanguard group, is one of the legendary figures of the investment business. In a keynote speech, "Investing with Simplicity," given in Philadelphia on October 3, 1998, Bogle made the following statement: "The realistic epitome of investment success is to realize the highest possible portion of the market returns earned in the financial asset class in which you invest—the stock market, the bond market, or the money market—recognizing and accepting that that portion will be less than 100 percent." One of the critical messages Bogle was trying to convey was that costs matter. In fact, because of their negative impact on returns, they matter a lot.

It is vital for investors to understand that the costs of trading fixed-income securities can be greatly affected by the manner, and market, in which they are traded. Most investors are probably not even aware that the bond market is actually made up of four distinct segments, each with its own unique characteristics. The unique characteristics have important cost implications for investors. There is the *primary* market and the *secondary* market. There is also the *interdealer* market (wholesale) and the *retail* market (end investor).

The Primary Market

Bonds that are purchased at issuance are said to trade in the *primary* market. The initial offering of a U.S. Treasury debt instrument is sold through an auction. Individual investors can participate in this process without incurring any transaction fee by establishing an account with the Federal Reserve Bank. This is done through what is called the TreasuryDirect program. This program, however, is available only for taxable accounts. Alternatively, Treasury issues can be purchased through banks or brokerages, in which case a modest fee of $25 to $50 is typically charged, regardless of the amount of the purchase.

The sales of the initial offering of corporate and municipal bonds are done differently. They are not sold directly to the public. Instead, they are sold to the public through an investment bank acting as what is known as an underwriter. Often groups of investment banks band together to form what is called a *syndicate* to buy the bonds. The syndicate then generally acts as part of a selling group that markets the bonds to the public. All bonds are sold at the same price. This is one reason why it is generally preferable for individual investors who do not have access to the interdealer market to buy individual bonds in the primary market—there is no markup or commission taken by the seller as the selling "concession" is paid for by the issuer. Thus individuals can be assured that they are getting the same price as large institutional investors.

The Secondary Market

Once the initial offering is completed any trading is then done in what is known as the *secondary* market. We begin by examining the secondary market for U.S. Treasury debt. The secondary market for Treasuries is the most liquid market in the world. In the wholesale (interbank or interdealer) market the typical trade is in blocks of $1 million and trades as large as $100 million are not uncommon. Just as is the case with equities, the prices of outstanding Treasury issues can be found in the *Wall Street Journal*. Thus prices can be said to be *transparent*. However, once we move beyond Treasuries, and enter the world of the secondary market for corporate and municipal bonds, the markets become *opaque*—at least at the retail level.

The Federal Reserve Flow of Funds report has estimated that while individual investors directly hold 40 percent of the market value of all corporate equities, they directly hold just 7 percent of the total market value of debt instruments. With institutions controlling 93 percent of the market, the technology related to information on pricing of fixed-income securities is designed for the institutional market. The technology that allows professional investors (both broker-dealers and fund managers) to follow market pricing in a timely manner is very expensive, and thus generally not available to the individual investor. The expense is so great that even most financial advisors do not have access to the pricing data. The result is that there is a large asymmetry of pricing knowledge between retail and institutional investors. This asymmetry has major implications for the prices that individuals pay.

Whenever there is a large asymmetry of pricing knowledge between retail and institutional buyers it is highly likely that the prices paid for the same product will vary greatly. An example of how an asymmetry of knowledge impacts prices paid is the diamond business. The markups between retail and wholesale prices paid for diamonds are typically very large. If you shop around, you will likely discover that diamonds of essentially the same quality (i.e., cut, clarity, weight, and color) are being sold by different retailers at vastly different prices. For example, if you happen to have a good friend who works in the diamond district in midtown Manhattan the price is likely to be dramatically lower than what it would be at most retailers. In any case, it is unlikely that the buyer will ever know the true wholesale price. Similarly, an asymmetry of knowledge has great implications for the prices that individuals pay when they buy securities. Consider the following.

When an individual buys shares in a company (e.g., Microsoft) whose stock is traded on one of the exchanges, she can buy that stock from any broker. She also can easily find out exactly what the bid and offer prices are for the stock at any given moment. The price at which the purchase will be executed is likely to be very similar, no matter which firm executes the trade on her behalf. The only difference might be the size of the commission. The transparency in pricing protects most investors from being exploited in terms of the price they pay. This is, unfortunately, not the case in the municipal bond market. Nor is it the case with corporate bonds, with the exception of the few corporate bonds that trade on the New York and American stock exchanges (NYSE and AMEX). Contributing to the transparency of prices is the centralized manner in which trading is conducted. The market for municipal bonds is a very decentralized one. It operates through an over-the-counter network of primary and regional dealers. The lack of centralization contributes to the lack of transparency in pricing.

There are other crucial differences between the secondary market for equities and the secondary market for bonds, especially municipal bonds. The first major difference, as we just discussed, is that while individuals directly hold about 40 percent of equities, they directly hold only about 7 percent of bonds.

The second major difference is that while stocks are traded very heavily in the secondary market (over a billion shares are typically traded daily on the NYSE alone) most municipal and corporate bonds are owned by buy-and-hold investors. Thus while the equity market is highly liquid (resulting in low trading costs), the market for municipal and corporate bonds is generally very illiquid. The lack of liquidity results in very high trading costs.

The lack of liquidity in the secondary market creates another difference between stocks and bonds. If you want to buy any particular stock, you can do so simply by calling a securities dealer. The situation is very different for municipal bonds. It is not likely that a dealer will actually be holding in inventory the specific bond you want. They will have to search the market to find someone who owns the bond. And they may not be successful. The more difficult a bond is to find, the greater the price you are likely to pay. Fortunately, this does not present much of a problem on the buy side since bonds (at least investment-grade bonds) of the same credit rating and maturity are highly likely to provide the same return. The problem, however, is that the lack of liquidity and transparency makes it very difficult to compare prices of securities of comparable rating and maturity. The liquidity and transparency issue becomes much more critical if you have to sell a municipal bond prior to maturity—you are likely to incur a significant cost in the form of a price concession (markdown or "haircut").

A third major difference is that the secondary market for individual stocks generally remains vibrant as long as a company is public. This is not the case with municipal bonds. The longer a bond is outstanding, the less frequently it tends to be traded. Some bonds may not trade for months or even years. Another related problem is that it may be very difficult to obtain the prospectus for a bond trading in the secondary market.

Finally, the sheer number of issues creates a problem in reporting the prices of municipal bonds traded in the secondary market. While there are about eight thousand stocks traded on the three major exchanges (NYSE, AMEX, and NASDAQ), it is estimated that there are about 50,000 issuers with over 1,700,000 individual municipal bond issues outstanding (more than all the public equity issues outstanding around the globe). According to the Municipal Securities Rulemaking Board (MSRB) only a tiny fraction (1,000 out of 1,700,000) of these issues trade on a daily basis. Only 10 percent of bonds that do trade on a given day trade as much as four times that day, and there is only a one in three chance of repeating that on the following day. They also estimate that less than 30 percent of municipal bonds will trade in any given year.

All of the above factors contribute to the high cost of trading municipal bonds. The lack of liquidity and the lack of transparency results in the deck being stacked against the individual investor—from the perspective of a broker-dealer, the individual investor is ripe for exploitation. This leads to the following conclusion: Only investors who know with a virtual certainty that they will be able to hold individual municipal bonds they purchase until maturity should even consider buying them. And individuals acting on their own should only buy them in the primary market (at the initial offering).

How Bonds Are Bought and Sold

To understand how bonds are traded we begin with an explanation of the bid-offer spread. The *bid* is the price at which you can sell a security, and the *offer* is the price you must pay to buy a security. The spread is the difference between the two prices. The size of the spread (the difference between the bid and the offer) is directly related to the riskiness of the bond from the dealer's perspective— the more (less) liquid the trading is in a particular bond, the smaller (greater) will be the spread. The size of the spread is also related to the riskiness of the credit—the weaker (stronger) the credit rating, the greater (smaller) the spread. A third factor impacting the size of the spread is the price volatility of the security—the greater (lesser) the volatility, the larger (smaller) the spread.

There are two other terms that we must define that relate to pricing. A *markup* is the amount the broker-dealer adds to the wholesale offer price when selling to the investor. A *markdown* (or haircut) is the amount the dealer subtracts from the wholesale bid price when buying from an investor. The pricing on a particular bond in the wholesale (interdealer) market might be quoted, for example, as 100–101. That means that the dealer's bid (the price at which he is willing to buy) is 100, and his offer (the price he is willing to sell) is 101. However, if the retail investor was interested in buying that same bond the broker-dealer might offer to sell the bond at a price of 103. The difference between the interdealer offer price of 101 and the retail offer price of 103 (2 points, or roughly 2 percent) reflects the dealer's markup. Alternatively, if the retail investor wished to sell that same bond the broker-dealer's bid might be just 98. The difference between the interdealer bid price of 100 and the retail bid price of 98 is the dealer's markdown. What determines the size of the markup and markdown? Several factors come into play.

The first factor impacting the size of the dealer markup or markdown is the riskiness of the bond. Just as the riskiness of a bond impacts the size of the spread, it also impacts the size of the markup or markdown. The riskiness of a bond from a dealer's perspective is related not only to its liquidity, but also to its price volatility. When a broker-dealer holds a bond in inventory he is taking price risk. Since long-term bonds are more risky than short-term bonds, the markup or markdown on longer-term bonds is likely to be greater—as compensation to the dealer for taking that incremental risk.

A second factor is the relative transparency of the market. The more opaque the market, the more the brokerage firm will be tempted to increase its profit on the trade. The reason is that the investor is unlikely to find out just how large a profit was taken—how much they were exploited. Because the market for Treasuries is so liquid, brokers have to be very careful when determining the size of their markup. However, when it comes to municipal bonds and mortgage-backed securities, the almost total lack of available pricing information provides a great temptation to widen spreads.

Size Matters

Another factor that determines the size of the spread is the size of the trade. For example, in the corporate market a $100,000 trade is considered to be a normal block size, while in the municipal market $50,000 would be considered to be a normal block. Trades that are smaller will have a larger markup or haircut (markdown) applied—the smaller the trade, the larger the impact on the price. Break points in terms of pricing can be expected at $1 million, $500,000, $250,000, $100,000, $50,000, $25,000, and below $25,000. An example will illustrate the impact of size on the cost of trading municipal bonds.

A municipal bond might exchange hands between dealers at 100 (i.e., at par). The dealer might offer to sell to a retail investor a block of $50,000 at a price of 102. If the buyer, however, was purchasing just $25,000 the offer price might now be 102.5. For an even smaller lot of just $10,000 the offer might be 103 or even 103.5. Conversely if the price were for a block of $250,000 the offer might be just 101.75, and for $500,000 the price might be 101.5. If another retail client wanted to sell that same bond to the dealer the bid for a block of $50,000 might be 98, dropping to as low as perhaps 97 or 96.5 for a lot of just $10,000.

Unfortunately, the MSRB provides almost no guidelines as to a limit on the amount a broker-dealer can mark the price of a bond up or down. The only guidance is what is known as Rule G-18. It requires that brokers trade at prices that are "fair and reasonable in relation to prevailing market conditions." Given that the makeup of the MSRB member board is five representatives from bank dealers, five representatives from securities firms, and just five representatives from the public, it is easy to see that any oversight is biased in favor of the industry, not the investor.

It is also unfortunate that the SEC does not require a broker-dealer to disclose the amount of markup or markdown charged. The result is that transactions costs in bond trades can be like icebergs, where the largest part (seven-eighths) is hidden beneath the surface. Because glacier ice is only slightly lighter than an equal amount of seawater, most of an iceberg remains below the waves. It is very dangerous for boats to travel in icy waters without equipment that can help them locate an iceberg.

When buying bonds, the danger is that because the only required disclosure is the transaction fee (which is not a commission, rather an administrative fee), most investors assume it is the only cost they will incur—typically a nominal amount such as $25 or $50. As we have seen, however, this is definitely not the case—it is just the tip of the iceberg. Without the assistance of the technology needed to identify markups and markdowns, investors may incur large costs of which they are not even aware.

Markups and markdowns can be very large, since there is little in the way of regulations to prevent abuses. We are sure the following will shock most investors.

In a May 2002 ruling, SEC administrative law Judge Lillian A. McEwen dismissed fraud charges brought by the SEC and the MSRB against a Los Angeles broker. McEwen concluded: "Markups and markdowns on municipal securities ranging from 1.87 to 5.64 percent were not excessive and did not violate the securities fraud laws."[1] To put this in context, Vanguard's bond funds carry operating expense ratios of only about 0.2 percent.

If those markups and markdowns don't shock you, how about these? The Web site MunicipalBonds.com reports each quarter on the one hundred worst municipal bond trades. The worst trades are defined by the size of the spread between the price a customer sold a bond to a dealer and the price another customer paid the dealer for that same bond. The worst trade reported during the second quarter of 2004 was a spread of *80 percent.* The spread on the one-hundredth worst trade was still in excess of 7 percent.

Although brokerage firms are legally allowed to charge undisclosed markups ranging upward of 5 percent, the practice is unfair because it takes advantage of investors who might not be aware that bonds commonly include markups from a broker-dealer (considering the markup charged may often be disproportionate to the riskiness of the bond's features). Whether legal or not, fees of this size are certainly not in the interest of the investor, and the failure to disclose them is an indication that broker-dealers would agree.

A dealer is entitled to a markup or markdown for the services they provide. However, its size should reflect the risk entailed. For example, if a broker were asked to bid on a risky and illiquid bond, then he would be entitled to a greater markdown than would otherwise be the case. On the other hand, if he were simply going to immediately resell that same bond into the secondary market, then only a very small markup would be appropriate. Unfortunately, the size of the spread may provide more insight into the integrity of the dealer than it does on the risk of the transaction.

Some Light Beginning to Shine Through

Fortunately for investors, some light is beginning to be shed on bond pricing. All municipal and corporate bonds, as well as all pass-through securities (such as mortgage-backed securities like GNMAs), are assigned a nine-digit CUSIP (Committee on Uniform Security Identification Process)—a means of identification. It is the equivalent of a stock symbol (all stocks also receive CUSIPs). CUSIPs allow market participants to track the price of bonds as they are bought and sold in both the wholesale (interdealer) and retail (investor) markets. Because all trades, and the prices at which they occurred, must be reported, those that have access to the technology can determine approximately what markup or markdown was added to the interdealer price. Bloomberg, a large financial media firm that provides financial data to participants in the securities markets, provides that service (as part of a package of related services) for a very substantial fee (about $20,000 per year). Investors can ask their broker-dealer to show them the prices at which the bond they bought or sold traded at on the day of their transaction (or the days surrounding the trade). Good luck getting that information. A more likely alternative is to find an unbiased (fee-only) investment advisor who can provide this information for you.

The Games Brokers Play—At Your Expense

In the classic fairy tale "Snow White and the Seven Dwarfs," the evil Queen, Snow White's jealous stepmother, arrives at Snow White's cottage disguised as an old peddler woman. Despite being warned by the seven dwarfs to not open the door for anyone or accept any gifts, Snow White answers the door. The Queen uses the girl's naïveté against her and lures Snow White into taking a bite from a poisoned apple. Falling into a sleeping death, Snow White can only be awakened by love's first kiss.

The moral of the story is that children should be wary of old ladies who come knocking at their door tempting them with treats. It is more than likely that the old lady has a hidden agenda. The broker dealer community knows that individual investors lack sufficient knowledge about the bond market, which makes exploiting them as easy as "taking candy from a baby." Unfortunately for those investors, Prince Charming will not be riding in on a white horse to save them or their portfolio. The following are just two examples of how brokers exploit the naïveté of investors.

The first example relates to the maturity of the bonds brokers prefer to sell. Investors need to be aware that the size of the impact of a markup or markdown on the yield of a bond is negatively related to its remaining term-to-maturity. For example, a bond with a remaining maturity of just one year will see a return impact of one percent for each one point of markup or markdown. However, the impact on yield is reduced as the term-to-maturity lengthens because the markup will be "amortized" over a longer time. Consider the following example.

A bond with a remaining term of just one year is yielding 3 percent and trading at par (100). A markup of even 1 percent would be very hard to hide, as the yield-to-maturity would drop by more than 1 percent to 1.98 percent. On the other hand, if the bond had a remaining term of ten years, the yield-to-maturity would fall to about 2.85 percent. That is a drop in yield of just 0.15 percent. And if the bond had a remaining term of twenty-five years the yield-to-maturity would fall to about 2.93 percent. That is a drop in yield of just 0.07 percent. The longer the maturity, the less the impact on yield-to-maturity and the easier it is to hide the markup. Now imagine a broker wanting to take a markup of four points on the same bond. That would be very hard to do with a bond with just one year remaining to maturity because the yield-to-maturity would then be negative—the investor would pay 104 for a bond that in one year would return his $100 in principal and just $3 of interest. On the other hand, the impact on the yield-to-maturity of a bond with twenty-five years to maturity would be only about thirty-one basis points (0.31 percent) per annum.

It isn't hard to guess which maturities brokers push when selling bonds to individual investors. Unfortunately, not only do investors end up paying large transaction fees, but they also end up taking far more price risk than would be typically prudent. (We will discuss the historical evidence on the relationship between risk and term-to-maturity in the next chapter.)

Another example of how brokers can exploit individual investors is by selling them premium bonds that have call dates that are much closer than the maturity date. The bonds sell at a premium as a result of their high coupons (the attraction) relative to current market rates. Again an example will illustrate how brokers can take advantage of the opaqueness of pricing and exploit an investor's lack of knowledge about bond pricing and the risks of fixed-income investing.

A bond with a remaining term-to-maturity of twenty-five years is carrying a coupon of 6 percent. The current market rate for similar bonds is now 4 percent and the bond can be called at 101 in one year. Despite the relatively high coupon (2 percent above the current market rate) and the long remaining term-to-maturity, the bond should not be trading much above the call price of 101 because of the nearness of the call date and the high likelihood that the bond will be called by the issuer. Let's assume the bond is trading at 103. Now the broker decides to add a markup of five points and sells the bond to the investor at 108. The broker might tell the investor that the yield-to-maturity is about 5.6 percent, well above current market rates. (Remember from our prior example how a long maturity can camouflage the size of the markup.) Unfortunately, the bond will almost certainly be called in one year. Assuming it is called at 101 the investor will have earned the coupon of 6 percent and lost seven points in price, producing a net loss of 1 percent. As you can see, the investor was actually sold a bond with a negative expected return! This is not as rare as you might think. But it gets worse. When the bond is called the broker will call the investor to advise him of the call. The investor now has to reinvest the cash and the broker gets to play the same game all over again.

A less extreme example would be if the call date were in three years instead of just one. In this case the price of the bond in the wholesale market would be around 106. With the same markup of five points the bond would be sold to the investor at 111. If the bond is called at 100 in three years, as is likely, then the investor would have earned a return of less than 3 percent (having earned the coupon of 6 percent but also having to amortize the premium of eleven points over just three years).

It is important to note that while the law does not require dealers to quote the yield-to-maturity, they are required to quote to the yield-to-worst. As you have seen, however, despite this requirement abuses occur. If you ever purchase an individual bond be sure that you ask the dealer to disclose both the yield-to-worst and the yield-to-maturity.

Beware of Greeks (or Brokers) Bearing Gifts

The expression "Beware of Greeks bearing gifts" is derived from the classical epic *The Iliad*, in which a large, hollow horse made of wood was used by the Greeks to defeat the Trojans. The resourceful Greeks hid soldiers inside the horse and left it outside the gates of Troy. They anchored their ships just out of sight of Troy and left a man behind to say that the goddess Athena would be pleased if the Trojans brought the horse inside the city and honored it. The Trojans took the bait, against the advice of Cassandra and Laocoön. That night the Greek army returned to Troy. The men inside the horse emerged and opened the city gates for their companions. The Greeks sacked the city, thus winning the war.

The investment equivalent of the Trojan horse is a broker bearing a gift in the form of a great bond for you to buy. A broker calls a customer, or potential customer, and says: "*We* have a unique opportunity to buy this great bond. It is a real bargain. I have to tell you that it won't be available for long." The broker concludes, "How much can I put you down for?"

If you ever hear a pitch like this, the first and only response you should make is to hang up. First, there are no great bargains in the bond market. Second, even if such a bargain existed you should ask yourself, "Why are they offering to sell it to *me* instead of to some large institutional client with whom they do millions, if not hundreds of millions, of dollars in business every year?" In all likelihood, the reality is that the trading desk of the brokerage firm wants to unload some bond that they no longer want to hold in inventory (and possibly for a very good reason, like the credit is deteriorating or the market is looking weak for similar securities). In order to move the bond as quickly as possible the trading desk will offer the brokers of the firm a larger concession (price discount to which the broker can then apply a markup) as an incentive to sell the bond. Typically the broker would then add his or her own markup to further increase his or her compensation. Great deal for the broker, lousy deal for the unsuspecting investor. Remember that when a broker says *we* have a great opportunity to *buy* a bond what he is really saying is that *he* has a great opportunity to *sell* a bond. *You* are doing the *buying,* not the broker!

One last point: In her book *The Bond Bible,* veteran money manager Marilyn Cohen recommends that whenever a broker calls with a recommendation on a bond and tells you that he just bought that security for himself (or his parents) be sure to ask for a copy of that confirmation slip. She describes this tactic as one of the most popular fibs. The same advice applies to recommendations to buy stocks or mutual funds. Whenever you get advice from brokers or financial advisors you should always ask to see their financial statement to see if they are investing in the same securities they are advising you to purchase—making sure that they are "putting their money where their mouth is."

The above examples illustrate how essential it is to be an educated investor. Hopefully they also have shown you that while education doesn't have to be expensive (consider the price of this book), ignorance can be very expensive when you have brokers who don't have their customers' best interests at heart.

We have now completed our discussion of how bonds are bought and sold. The next chapter focuses on how the academic community believes the fixed-income markets really work—how markets set security prices. We will also explore the relationship between risk and reward. Keep in mind that most investors obtain their "knowledge" of how markets work from Wall Street and the financial media. This is, unfortunately, the equivalent of getting medical advice from *People* magazine. Learning how the academic community believes markets work, on the other hand, is the equivalent of getting medical advice from the rigorously peer-reviewed *New England Journal of Medicine.* The knowledge we gain will lead us to the winning investment strategy.

CHAPTER FOUR

◆

How the Fixed-Income
Markets Really Work

Basically, we were guessing on interest rates. What we've come to believe is that no one can guess interest rates.
  —Fred Henning, head of fixed-income investing at Fidelity Investments, quoted in the *Los Angeles Times*, July 22, 1997

Today's investors find it inconceivable that life might be better without so much information. Investors find it hard to believe that ignoring the vast majority of investment noise might actually improve investment performance. The idea sounds too risky because it is so contrary to their accepted and reinforced actions.
  —Richard Bernstein, first vice president and chief quantitative strategist at Merrill Lynch

The most costly of all follies is to believe passionately in the palpably not true.   —H. L. Mencken

There are two general theories about how markets work. The first, which is the *conventional wisdom* (because it is accepted by almost all investors), is that there are smart people working hard who can uncover securities that have been somehow mispriced by the market. In the case of equities (stocks) that means that there are people who can identify which stocks are undervalued or overvalued, and there are also people who can identify when the bear is about to emerge from its hibernation (it's time to get out of the market) and when the bull is about to start another rampage (it's time to jump in and get fully invested). The former is the art of stock selection and the latter is the art of market timing. Together they form the practice of active management.

When it comes to fixed-income investing the same two active management strategies can be employed. Timing the market would involve guessing when interest rates are going to rise (you would sell longer-term instruments and buy shorter-term ones) or fall (the reverse strategy would be used). Security selection would entail identifying which securities are mispriced (under- or overvalued) by the market. For example, a security might be rated A by the major rating agencies (Standard & Poor's, Moody's, and Fitch), yet an analyst might decide that it really deserves a AA rating and it will be upgraded when the agencies figure it out (get it right). The analyst, therefore, would recommend the bond for purchase because, if an upgrade in credit rating were to occur, the price of the bond would be expected to rise and a profit could be made.

Investors need to understand that just because something is conventional wisdom does not make it correct. For example, "The earth is flat" was once conventional wisdom. As author Nicholas Chamfort noted: "There are well-dressed foolish ideas just as there are well-dressed fools."

Another great, and perhaps more relevant, example of conventional wisdom being wrong is the case of Galileo, the Italian astronomer who lived in the sixteenth and seventeenth centuries. He spent the last eight years of his life under house arrest, a punishment ordered by the Roman Catholic Church for committing the "crime" of believing in and teaching the doctrines of Copernicus. Galileo's conflict with the Church arose because he was fighting the accepted doctrine that the earth was the center of the universe. Ptolemy, a Greek astronomer, had proposed this theory in the second century. It went unchallenged until 1530 when Copernicus published his major work, *On the Revolution of Celestial Spheres,* which stated that the earth rotated around the sun rather than the other way around. The example of Galileo demonstrates that even when millions of people believe a foolish thing it is still a foolish thing. As Don Marquis, writer, poet, and journalist, noted, "An idea is not responsible for the people who believe in it."

People cling to the infallibility of an idea even when there is overwhelming evidence that the idea has no basis in reality— particularly when a powerful establishment finds it in its interest to resist change. In Galileo's case, the establishment was the Church. In the case of the belief in active management, the establishment comprises Wall Street, most of the mutual fund industry, and the financial media. All of them would make far less money if investors were fully aware of the failure of active management. This brings us to the second theory on how markets work.

The Efficient Market Hypothesis

The foundation of the second theory is what is called the *efficient market hypothesis* (EMH). The following is a very simple definition of the EMH: Prices of securities traded in the public market are the best available estimates of their real value because of the highly efficient pricing mechanism inherent in the market. If this is true, then the conventional wisdom must be wrong.

The EMH is based on over fifty years of academic research on how capital markets work. Here is what Michael C. Jensen, Harvard professor of business administration, had to say about the EMH: "There is no other proposition in economics that has more solid empirical evidence supporting it than the efficient market hypothesis. In the literature of finance, accounting, and the economics of uncertainty, the EMH is accepted as a fact of life."[1]

If markets are efficient, which is one of the fundamental tenets of the investment strategy recommended in this book, active management is not likely to be able to add value after the expenses of the efforts are deducted. The reason is that the market price is, as Jensen stated, the best *estimate* of the correct price. If another price were the best estimate, the market would quote that price instead.

There are two important issues related to the EMH that often confuse investors. The first is that the EMH does not preclude the *possibility* that some investors will outperform the market. Instead, it says that there is no way for investors to identify ahead of time who the few that might do so will be. As you will see, relying, for example, on past successful performance simply doesn't work. There is no way, therefore, to identify *ahead of time* the future winners. And, unfortunately, we can only buy future returns, not past returns.

The second mistaken notion people have about the EMH is that it does *not* preclude the possibility of the market being wrong. For example, it might turn out that the market might have been overly optimistic about the outlook for interest rates (and thus rates were "too low"). The problem is that there is no evidence that *after accounting for expenses* there are investors who can persistently exploit any such pricing errors. Markets can be irrationally exuberant or irrationally pessimistic. However, unless investors can exploit such irrationality the market can be said to be efficient. Active managers not only have to cover the cost of their research, but they also must add enough value to cover all trading costs. In addition, for taxable accounts they would have to add enough value to cover the increased taxes that are often generated from their increased trading activity.

Unfortunately for investors who believe in the conventional

wisdom (that active management is likely to add value), there is a body of overwhelming evidence that suggests that the markets, both for equities and bonds, are in fact highly efficient. For example, Mark M. Carhart's study on equity mutual fund performance analyzed 1,892 funds for the period 1962–93. He found that the average equity fund underperformed its appropriate style benchmark by about 1.8 percent per annum on a pretax basis. Carhart also found no evidence of any persistence in outperformance beyond the randomly expected (though he did find some persistence among the worst performers).[2] There are now probably hundreds of studies on the subject and they basically come to the same conclusion—the markets are highly efficient. Even those researchers that conclude the markets are not perfectly efficient often suggest that investors are best served if they act as if they were—because the costs of trying to exploit inefficiencies are likely to exceed the benefits.

Consider what the American Law Institute had to say about market efficiency when in 1992 it wrote the Third Restatement of the Prudent Investor Rule. After looking at the evidence they concluded that:

"Economic evidence shows that, from a typical investment perspective, the major capital markets of this country are *highly efficient,* in the sense that available information is rapidly digested and reflected in the market prices of securities.

"As a result, fiduciaries and other investors are confronted with potent evidence that the application of expertise, investigation, and diligence in efforts to 'beat the market' in these publicly traded securities ordinarily promises little or no payoff, or even a negative payoff after taking account of research and transaction costs.

"Empirical research supporting the theory of efficient markets reveals that in such markets skilled professionals have rarely been able to identify underpriced securities (that is, to outguess the market with respect to future return) with any regularity.

"In fact, evidence shows that there is little correlation between fund managers' earlier successes and their ability to produce above-market returns in subsequent periods."[3]

In his excellent book, *The Prudent Investor Act* (a must read for anyone with trustee responsibilities as well as for anyone managing their own assets), W. Scott Simon reached the conclusion that under the Uniform Prudent Investor Act, which sets forth standards that govern the investment activities of trustees, and is currently the law in most states, "passive investing (e.g., index and [passive] asset class funds) appears to be the standard for investing and managing trust portfolios."[4]

The Evidence on Market Efficiency

The following are the results of just two of the many studies that could be cited on the attempts of active management to exploit market inefficiencies in the fixed-income markets. A study covering as many as 361 bond funds showed that the average actively managed bond fund underperforms its benchmark index by 0.85 percent per annum.[5] Another study found that only 128 (16 percent) out of 800 fixed-income funds beat their relevant benchmark over the ten-year period covered.[6] Of course, being a loser's game does not mean there are not some winners. That leaves the hope that we can identify the few winners ahead of time. Unfortunately, the evidence suggests that believing so would be the triumph of hope over experience. For example, John Bogle of Vanguard studied the performance of bond funds and concluded that "although past absolute returns of bond funds are a flawed predictor of future returns, there is a fairly easy way to predict future relative returns." Bogle found that "the superior funds could have been systemically identified based solely on their lower expense ratios."[7] Other studies on the subject, including those on municipal bond funds, all reach the same conclusions:

- Past performance cannot be used to predict future performance.

- Actively managed funds do not, on average, provide value added in terms of returns.

- The major cause of underperformance is expenses—there is a consistent one-for-one negative relationship between expense ratios and net returns.

The results of a study by Morningstar demonstrate both the importance of costs and that the past performance of actively managed funds is a poor predictor of future performance. They tested funds with strong performance and high costs against those with poor past performance with low costs. "Sure enough, those with low costs outperformed in the following period."[8]

Why did all these studies come to the conclusion that bond fund managers charge Georgia O'Keeffe prices and deliver paint-by-numbers results? The EMH provides the answer: The market's efficiency prevents active managers from persistently exploiting any mispricing. And as difficult as it is for active managers to add value when it comes to equity investing, it is much harder for them to add value in fixed-income investing. Let's see why this is true.

First, as we have already discussed, with U.S. Treasury debt, all bonds of the same maturity will provide the same return (with the exception of a few bonds that have call provisions). Thus, there will be no differentiation in performance, and, therefore, no ability to add value via security selection. If we restrict holdings to the highest investment grades, there is an extremely limited ability to add value via security selection (because credit risk is very low). That leaves interest rate forecasting as the only way an active manager might add value in any significant way. William Sherden, author of the wonderful book *The Fortune Sellers,* reviewed the leading research on forecasting accuracy from 1979 to 1995 and covering forecasts made from 1970 to 1995. He concluded that:

- *Economists cannot predict the turning points in the economy.* He found that of the forty-eight predictions made by economists, forty-six missed the turning points.
- *The forecasting skill of economists is about as good as guessing.* Even the economists who can directly or indirectly influence the economy (the Federal Reserve, the Council of Economic Advisors, and the Congressional Budget Office) had forecasting records that were worse than pure chance.
- *There are no economic forecasters who consistently lead the pack in forecasting accuracy.*
- *Consensus forecasts do not improve accuracy.*[9]

Michael Evans, founder of Chase Economics, confessed: "The problem with macro [economic] forecasting is that no one can do it."[10] Since the underlying basis of interest rate forecasts is an economic forecast, the evidence suggests that bond market strategists who predict bull and bear markets will have no greater success than do the economists. If active managers are highly unlikely to add value via either security selection or market timing, the only conclusions we can draw are that the conventional wisdom is wrong and that the markets are highly efficient.

Once we conclude that the market is efficient, the winning strategy becomes obvious: It pays to be a passive buy-and-hold investor using only low-cost investment vehicles to implement the investment plan. The only question remaining is which instruments we should invest in. In order to determine the answer, we need to understand what the major determinants of fixed-income risk and expected return are.

The Two-Factor Fixed-Income Model

In 1977 Bill James self-published the book *1977 Baseball Abstract: Featuring 18 Categories of Statistical Information That You Just Can't Find Anywhere Else.* Seventy-five people found the book of sufficient interest to buy it.[11] Today James's annual edition (now called *The Bill James Handbook*) is considered a must read for all serious fans of our national pastime.

James demonstrated, through vigorous research, that certain statistics are more crucial than others in determining the effectiveness of a player. Among his many findings: A player's batting average and the number of home runs he hits are not as important as people have assumed. James found that other statistics were more vital, namely, the total of a player's on base percentage and his slugging average.

What James did was nothing less than revolutionize the way people think about baseball statistics and how to build a winning team. In fact, most teams today have statistical experts (called sabermaticians) on their staffs. Michael Lewis's book *Moneyball* explains how Billy Beane, the general manager of the Oakland Athletics, used sabermaticians to build a winning team despite the constraint of having a very limited payroll.

Just as James revolutionized the way we think about the game of baseball by assessing which factors were the most significant in determining the impact a player had on the outcome of a game, the publication of the paper "The Cross-Section of Expected Stock Returns," by professors Eugene F. Fama and Kenneth R. French, in the *Journal of Finance* in June 1992 had a dramatic impact on the field of financial economics. The Fama-French research produced what has become known as the three-factor model, and it explains virtually all (as much as 97 percent) of the variability in returns of diversified U.S. stock portfolios.

The conclusion that can be drawn from the Fama-French research is that the markets are efficient and, therefore, the vast majority of the returns one can expect from a diversified equity portfolio are unrelated to the ability either to pick stocks or to time the market. Instead, it is the degree of exposure to what Fama and French called *risk factors* that determines almost all of the variability in returns. The first risk factor in the three-factor equity model is the amount of exposure of a portfolio to the risk factor of the overall stock market. All equities have some exposure to this risk factor. Since equities are riskier than fixed-income investments, they provide greater *expected* returns. The second risk factor is the size of a company as determined by market capitalization. Intuitively we know that small companies are riskier than large companies—and they must provide greater *expected* returns. The third risk factor takes value into consideration. High book-to-market (value) stocks are intuitively riskier than low book-to-market (growth) stocks—and they must provide greater *expected* returns.

Thanks to professors Fama and French we have a similar two-factor model to explain the returns of fixed-income portfolios. The two risk factors are term and default (credit risk). The longer the term-to-maturity, the greater the risk, and the lower the credit rating, the greater the risk. And the markets compensate investors for taking risk with higher *expected* returns. Note that individual security selection and market timing do not play a significant role in explaining returns, and thus should not be expected to add value. If they did explain returns, then we would see evidence that active managers were adding value, not subtracting it.

The implication for investors is that the winning strategy in fixed-income markets, whether taxable or tax-exempt, is to choose the lowest-cost fund (and passive funds are likely to be the lowest cost) that meets your credit and maturity criteria. Alternatively, if your portfolio is large enough, and you can do so at a very low cost, the winning strategy is to build your own individually tailored portfolio. Note that for U.S. government securities mutual funds do not provide one of their greatest benefits, the diversification of risk (since U.S. Treasury securities have no credit risk). Thus building your own portfolio might be a good alternative.

With corporate and tax-exempt issues, however, credit risk is a consideration. That means that corporate and tax-exempt municipal bond funds do provide the benefit of diversification. Therefore, only those investors with portfolios large enough to achieve effective diversification (e.g., $500,000) should attempt to construct their own portfolios. In addition, because trading costs in the corporate and municipal bond markets are much greater than they are in the Treasury bond market, only investors who are almost certain that they will be able to buy and hold to maturity should own individual bonds.

Term Risk and Return

Academic research has found that over long periods of time, while investors have been compensated for accepting the risk of owning longer-maturity fixed-income assets, this relationship has broken down beyond two to three years. Research on the relationship between risk and return has shown that for the period 1964–2003:[12]

- Holding one-month short-term U.S. Treasury bills provides a risk-free rate of return (historically about 6.3 percent) and has an annual standard deviation of just over 1 percent.
- Extending the maturity to one year increases returns above the risk-free rate by about 1 percent while increasing the standard deviation to 2.4 percent.
- Extending the maturity to five years adds to returns only another 0.65 percent (total premium above the risk-free rate of about 1.7 percent), yet the standard deviation increases by more than two and one half times to 6.3 percent. Extending the maturity to twenty years causes returns to *fall* about 0.1 percent (total premium above the risk-free rate of about 1.6 percent), yet the standard deviation almost *doubles* again to 11.1 percent.

An important question for investors is how to determine the most efficient maturity in terms of return *relative* to risk. Nobel Prize–winner William Sharpe provided the answer when he developed what has become known as the Sharpe ratio.

The Sharpe ratio is a measure of return relative to risk. It is derived by first subtracting the average rate of return on riskless one-month Treasury bills from the average annual rate of return earned on the asset, then dividing the result by the standard deviation of the asset. The higher the Sharpe ratio, the more efficient is the investment in delivering returns relative to risk. The Sharpe ratio has been about 0.40 at the one-year maturity but falls to about 0.26 if we extend the maturity to about five years, and it continues to fall as we extend the maturity. Thus holding assets with a maturity of about one to two years is the prudent strategy for those investors wishing to maximize the risk-reward relationship. Note, however, that there may also be other considerations (to be discussed later) that should be taken into account in determining the term risk one is willing to take, including whether one is in the accumulation or withdrawal phase of one's investment life cycle.

It is important to note that the yield curve for municipal bonds is almost always steeper than it is for Treasuries. There are three basic reasons for this difference. Perhaps the one of greatest significance is that there is a greater supply of long-term bonds from issuers than there is demand for long-term municipal securities from investors. Municipalities are generally trying to match their liabilities with the long-term nature of their assets (e.g., highways, bridges, buildings, parks). On the other hand, most investor demand is for securities with short to intermediate maturities. In order for the market to absorb all the supply, prices adjust downward (yields rise). The two other factors that cause the municipal bond curve to be steeper than the Treasury curve are the credit risk of municipal securities and the potential for the loss of their tax-exempt status.

To illustrate the differences in the slopes of the different curves consider the following: If a five-year municipal bond were trading at 80 percent of a Treasury note with the same maturity, a ten-year municipal bond might trade at 85 percent, and a twenty-year municipal bond might trade at 90 percent. The result is that the risk-reward relationship for extending the maturity of an investment is better in the municipal bond market. The higher yield may make it attractive to consider longer maturities than would be the case for Treasuries or corporate bonds. Therefore, depending on the shape of the municipal bond yield curve at the time the investment decision is made, it may be appropriate to extend the maturity of municipal bonds perhaps to an average of about five to seven years (versus the one to two years for taxable instruments).

At this point we need to ask the question: If long-term bonds are riskier than short-term ones, and the market is efficient at pricing for risk, why have investors in long-term bonds not been compensated for the greater risk they have taken (using standard deviation as a measure of risk)? There is a good explanation for this seeming risk-return anomaly—while standard deviation is *a* measure of risk, it is not the only one. When thinking about risk, some investors care about issues other than volatility. There are many investors, such as pension plans, that have fixed long-term obligations. Insurance companies are another good example of investors who have relatively well defined long-term obligations. In order to create a match between the term of their defined liabilities (the pension obligations due to past and current employees) and the term of their assets (thereby *eliminating* risk), pension plans are willing to accept the interim price risk of the assets themselves. Now let's consider an alternative strategy.

To eliminate the price risk of holding long-term bonds, a pension plan buys three-month Treasury bills and continually rolls them over until they are needed to fund obligations. While there will be virtually no volatility in the price of their holdings, because the rate of return that will be earned over the long term is unknown, the pension plan would be running a great risk as to its ability to earn a return sufficient to fund its obligations. The result is that the investor demand for longer-maturity bonds exceeds the demand by issuers for liabilities of that length. Prices rise (and yields fall) when demand exceeds supply. In this case, the price of long-term bonds has risen sufficiently to make them bad investments for those investors not needing them to match a liability of similar length. Note that since these pension plans are not buyers of municipal bonds, this does not apply to the municipal bond yield curve.

There is another reason to consider not owning longer-term fixed-income instruments, especially if you are in the accumulation phase of investing. During the accumulation phase the main reason for holding fixed-income assets is generally to provide a safety net to anchor your portfolio during bear markets, allowing you to stay disciplined. In order for the safety net to be effective, the assets it holds must have low correlation with the risky equity portion of the portfolio. Unfortunately, the longer the maturity, the higher the correlation of fixed-income assets to equities. Also, unfortunately, that higher correlation with the equity portion of your portfolio can appear at just the wrong time. There may be times when interest rates rise, bond prices fall, and the stock market falls at the same time. Just when you need low correlation, you may get high correlation. The following are the correlations between Treasury instruments of various maturities and the S&P 500 and EAFE indices.[13] Remember that the lower the correlation, the more effective the diversification, and the lower the overall risk of the portfolio. Note also that there is basically no correlation between short-term maturities (up to one year) and

Annual Correlation Data

Maturity	Correlation with S&P 500 Index 1964–2003	Correlation with EAFE Index 1969–2003
One month	0.02	−0.11
Six months	0.03	−0.11
One year	0.05	−0.18
Five years	0.20	−0.02
Twenty years	0.26	0.09

Source: Dimensional Fund Advisors

U.S. equities and no correlation for up to five years between short-term maturities and international equities.

As the above figures demonstrate, the risk of having relatively higher correlation between equities and fixed-income instruments can be avoided by buying short-term fixed-income instruments— they have essentially no correlation with equities.

The Prudent Strategy

With the preceding information, we can determine that for those investors using fixed-income assets to reduce the risk of an equity portfolio the prudent strategy is to own only very short-term fixed-income assets of the highest investment quality. Here's why.

Since the main purpose of fixed-income assets is to reduce the volatility of the overall portfolio, investors should include fixed-income assets that have low volatility. Short-term fixed-income assets have both low volatility and low correlation with the equity portion of the portfolio. By limiting the maturity of the fixed-income portion of the portfolio to just one year, we get most of the yield benefit and accept only moderate risk (a standard deviation of only 2 percent). The benefit of lower volatility of the asset class itself, combined with the benefit of the reduced volatility of the overall portfolio, seems a small price to pay for giving up the extra thirty basis points in annual returns that have been gained by extending the maturity of the fixed-income assets to five years. Remember, in a 60 percent equity and 40 percent fixed-income portfolio, that extra thirty basis points (0.3 percent) becomes an added return on the overall portfolio of only twelve basis points per annum (0.3 percent × 40 percent).

We can further improve on this scenario by including international short-term fixed-income assets within the fixed-income allocation (as long as the assets are hedged against currency risk).

The reason is that their inclusion should further reduce volatility, since not all international fixed-income markets fluctuate in the same direction at the same time or by the same amount. The lack of perfect correlation will reduce the overall volatility of the fixed-income portion of the portfolio. The subject of international fixed-income securities is covered in depth in chapter 8.

A Shifting-Maturity Approach to Fixed-Income Investing

There is another fixed-income investment strategy (instead of buying and holding) that is based on the research of Eugene F. Fama and Robert R. Bliss. Their study "The Information in Long-Maturity Forward Rates," published in the September 1987 edition of the *American Economic Review,* covered the period from 1964 through 1985 and examined the historical returns of Treasury instruments with maturities out to five years.

Fama and Bliss concluded that today's yield curve contains information about future yield curves—current forward rates provide the best forecast of future spot interest rates. In other words, today's yield curve is the best estimate we have of what future yield curves will be. For example, if today's yield on a five-year Treasury note is 5 percent, at any point in the future the best estimate of what the five-year Treasury yield will be is also 5 percent—our best estimate is that the yield curve will not change over time. They also found that the longer the horizon, the greater the forecasting power contained in today's yield curve.

The results found by Fama and Bliss are in direct conflict with the expectations theory of the term structure of interest rates—that yields on Treasuries of different maturities are related primarily

73

by market expectations of future yields. In other words, the yield of a long-term bond will equal the average of the expected short-term interest rates over the same period. Fama and Bliss provided us with not only a better explanation, but also with insights that can help us improve on market returns.

Let's assume that, based on academic research, we have determined that we want to limit our fixed-income investments to a maturity of two years. After checking our Bloomberg screen we see that a one-month Treasury bill is yielding 1 percent, a U.S. Treasury note with a term-to-maturity of one year is yielding 2 percent, and a similar instrument with a two-year term-to-maturity is yielding 3 percent. Our investment choices would seem to be to buy:

1. The one-month bill and earn 1 percent for the first month and then repeat the process over the next twenty-three months.

2. The one-year note and earn 2 percent the first year and then repeat the process for the second year.

3. The two-year instrument and earn 3 percent.

If we had a clear crystal ball that could correctly forecast interest rates we would know which choice would prove to be the best. This is mostly what active management of fixed-income portfolios attempts to do. If we knew rates were about to fall sharply we would choose alternative 3. If we thought rates would rise sharply in the near future we would choose alternative 1. Unfortunately, as we have seen, all interest-rate forecasting balls are very cloudy. However, Fama and Bliss's work suggests a strategy with an alternative approach. The strategy is based upon the information contained in the current yield curve.

Instead of buying and holding the two-year instrument until maturity we can consider buying the two-year note and selling it in one year to buy another two-year note, which could then be sold after holding it for one year. What rate of return can we expect to earn by executing this strategy? The Fama and Bliss study tells us how to estimate that rate. Note that to keep the example as simple as possible the following calculations ignore the effect of compounding.

If the current two-year rate is 3 percent, and the current one-year rate is 2 percent, then the one-year forward rate (the one-year rate one year from today) must be 4 percent (ignoring compounding effects). The math is simple. In order to earn 3 percent for the full two years, if we earn only 2 percent for the first year, the second year we must earn 4 percent ([2 percent + 4 percent] / 2 = 3 percent). Before proceeding, it is important to note that under the expectations theory of interest rates we would conclude the best forecast of the one-year rate one year from today would be 4 percent. Fama and Bliss showed this to be incorrect. Instead, the best estimate of what the one-year rate will be one year from today is the current one-year rate of 2 percent. The higher one-year forward rate at 4 percent is not a forecast of higher interest rates in the future. Instead, it is a risk premium. In this case the risk is term risk.

Returning to our example, let's see how it works if the current yield curve remains unchanged—the best assumption we can make. We buy the two-year instrument which today is yielding 3 percent. If we hold it for one year we will have earned 3 percent for that year. Now there is only one year left to maturity. Our assumption is that the then current one-year note will be yielding 2 percent (the best estimate of tomorrow's yield curve is today's). Since we will be holding an instrument with one year left to maturity yielding 3 percent, we could sell that instrument at a 1 percent profit. Our total return for the first year would have been 4 percent. We could then buy the two-year note again and repeat the process, again earning 4 percent.

The shifting-maturity approach finds the point on the yield curve that provides the greatest total return and invests in securities with that maturity, shifting maturities as the yield curve shifts. Dimensional Fund Advisors (DFA), which has successfully utilized this approach since 1983 for their fixed-income funds, adds two caveats to the strategy. The first is when considering shifting maturities, any trading costs must be accounted for. The second is that because longer-maturity bonds have more price risk, DFA imposes an arbitrary rule that a longer maturity must provide at least twenty basis points per annum in higher expected returns in order for DFA to extend the maturity. In other words, if in the above example the one-year bond had an expected return of 2 percent and the two-year of only 2.1 percent, then DFA, because they could expect to earn only an additional 0.1 percent (ten basis points), would not extend the maturity an additional year. In bondspeak this process is called "finding the sweet spot" on the yield curve. The sweet spot is the point at which the yield curve begins to bend sharply to the right—the curve begins to rapidly flatten out, no longer rising at a rate of at least twenty basis points per annum. Note that if the yield curve were either perfectly flat (all yields along the curve were the same) or inverted, the sweet spot would be one month. The more positively sloped the curve, the farther out will be the sweet spot.

What we have learned is that by adopting this very specific shifting-maturity approach investors can expect to earn higher returns than a simple passive or indexing strategy to fixed-income investments would provide. While individual investors are not able to actively trade the yield curve on a daily basis, they can apply a similar strategy. For example, Vanguard offers a short-term, an intermediate-term, and a long-term bond fund. Vanguard publishes the average maturity of their funds, allowing us to employ a shifting-maturity strategy. Let's see how this would work. Let's assume that the average maturity of the three Vanguard funds is two, five, and eight years, respectively. Applying our rule of thumb, we would buy the fund with the highest yield, as long as it met the criteria of providing at least twenty basis points of extra yield for each year of extra maturity (due to the tax-exemption available on municipal bonds, the hurdle rate to extend would be perhaps just fifteen basis points). Thus if the intermediate fund, with a maturity of five years, yielded at least sixty basis points (twenty basis points times three years) more than the short-term fund whose maturity is just two years, we would invest in the intermediate fund. If it did not yield at least an additional sixty basis points, we would invest in the shorter fund. We would also compare the yields of the long-term and intermediate fund and do the same mathematical comparison. Investors might perform the comparison on a quarterly basis, and shift accordingly. Investors building their own portfolios of individual bonds can, in theory, also consider doing the same thing. However, in the real world, trading costs at the retail level would likely more than destroy any benefit.

Before considering implementing this strategy you should carefully weigh the consequences of increasing maturity (going farther out on the curve). First, like any strategy it involves risks. While it has produced above-benchmark returns over the long run, it has not outperformed every year. Therefore, discipline is required. Second, if you invest in longer maturities, you will earn higher expected returns, but remember, you are also increasing the correlation of those returns to the equity portion of the portfolio, thus increasing the risk of the overall portfolio (not just the risk of the fixed-income assets).

Credit Risk and Reward

As we have discussed, with fixed-income investments there are two main risks for which investors should expect to be rewarded (a third risk is that of liquidity, the purchasing of less liquid assets). These risks are the risk of interest rate changes negatively impacting the value of the asset (duration, or term risk) and credit risk. We also noted that since the main purposes of fixed-income investing (beyond providing liquidity for short-term cash needs and unanticipated expenses) are to either reduce the overall risk of a portfolio or to provide a sure and stable cash flow, trying to enhance returns by taking significant credit risk would not be a prudent strategy. Note that the taking of liquidity risk, on the other hand, might be appropriate if that is a risk with which you are not concerned—if, say, you are virtually certain you will be able to hold the securities purchased until maturity. As we have discussed, if this is the case, the liquidity premium might be viewed as a free stop at the dessert tray.

The following table presents the results of the study "Which Risks Have Been Best Rewarded?" The results of the study support our conclusion that the prudent strategy is to limit maturities to the short to intermediate term and to also limit the taking of credit risk to the highest investment grades. The data is consistent with longer-term historical results presented earlier in this chapter.[14] The study covers the relatively brief period 1985–2002, so we have to be careful about drawing conclusions that might only be period specific.

We can make the following observations from the data.

- Extending maturities led to higher returns but produced a much greater increase in risk. For example, extending the maturity of Treasuries from 1–3 years to 7–10 years led to

Has Credit Risk Been Rewarded?

Asset Class	Mean Return	Standard Deviation
1–3 Year Treasuries	7.3%	1.9
1–3 Year AAA/AA Corporate Bonds	7.9%	1.8
1–3 Year A/BBB	8.0%	1.9
7–10 Year Treasuries	9.6%	6.5
7–10 Year AAA/AA	9.6%	5.7
7–10 Year A/BBB	9.6%	5.3
7–10 Year High-Yield Bonds	8.8%	7.7

U.S. Treasuries have no credit risk. AAA/AA are bonds of the highest investment grade. Bonds rated A/BBB are bonds with the lowest rating that are still considered of investment grade. High-yield bonds are often referred to as junk bonds.

an increase in returns of 32 percent, but volatility (one measure of risk) more than tripled. For AAA and AA bonds, returns increased 22 percent while volatility tripled. For A and BBB bonds, returns increased 20 percent while volatility almost tripled. In addition, as we have discussed, when you extend the maturity of fixed-income investments, you also increase their correlation with the equity holdings in your portfolio (increasing the risk of the overall portfolio because of the reduced diversification benefit).

• Taking credit risk was rewarded, but only in the short end of the yield curve. Investment-grade bonds provided higher returns than Treasuries, and did so without any increase in volatility. Note, however, that when we consider longer-term bonds this was not true. Investment-grade bonds did not provide any increase in returns over Treasuries, and they did exhibit slightly lower volatility. High-yield bonds, however, actually provided lower returns while exhibiting greater volatility.

When considering this data, because the results might be period specific, we should also consider the following:

- The period 1985 through 2002 was one of the greatest bull markets ever for long-term bonds. For example, the yield on ten-year Treasuries fell from almost 12 percent to under 4 percent. Despite this drop, long-term bonds produced lower risk-adjusted returns than shorter-term instruments.

- The period was one of the best for U.S. economic performance with no serious recession like that of the Great Depression or the one experienced in 1973–74. This should have been a period when credit risk was highly rewarded. However, the period does end with high-yield spreads at very high levels from a historic perspective. And spreads did retreat significantly beginning in 2003.

- Investors can invest in Treasuries at very little cost. Individuals can buy either a very low cost index fund to match the maturity they seek or they can buy bonds directly from the Treasury, saving a fund management fee. And since Treasuries do not carry any credit risk the main benefit of a mutual fund, diversification, is not needed.

- While corporate bonds carry higher interest rates than do government issues, credit losses and call features can offset the incremental yield. Treasury bonds generally do not have call features. In addition, the cost of running a mutual fund for corporate debt is likely to be much greater. First, trading costs will be greater because part of the incremental yield is a premium for the lower level of trading liquidity in corporate bonds; and the lower the credit rating, the less the liquidity (and the greater the trading costs). Second, it is likely that the operating expenses of the fund will be greater due to expenditures incurred to analyze credit risks.

- Moving from Treasury instruments to corporate instruments increases the correlation with the equities in your portfolio, which negatively impacts the portfolio from a diversification and risk perspective. And the lower the credit rating of the corporate bond, the greater the negative impact.

In summary, the historical evidence suggests that, from an overall portfolio perspective, investors in fixed-income securities are best rewarded for taking risk if they adopt the following strategies:

- Extend maturities beyond one-month but remain in the short to intermediate part of the yield curve.
- If credit risk is taken, invest at the highest investment grade and stick to the shorter end of the curve.

Investors in the Withdrawal Stage

It is important to note that for individuals in the withdrawal stage of investing the recommendation to limit maturities to the short to intermediate part of the yield curve may not be the most appropriate strategy. For investors who have recurring cash flow or income needs, exposure to constantly changing rates (from remaining at the short end of the yield curve) may introduce larger risks to the portfolio in the form of funding shortfalls than the price risks introduced to the portfolio from extending maturities. This is true particularly in cases where the nominal liability stream being funded is relatively well defined and inflexible, and the investor's intent is to hold bonds to maturity. Thus an investor heavily dependent upon cash flows emanating from their investment portfolio could conclude that the risk of changing interest rates is greater than the risks of more volatile price swings. For these investors a measure of risk such as the Sharpe ratio may not be the most appropriate.

Just as a contractor must have the appropriate tools for each job, investors must know which analytical tools are appropriate for their situation. Using the wrong tools to fix a plumbing problem could result in leaks and water damage. Using the wrong tools to assess the health of your portfolio could result in poor outcomes.

Investors who do choose to extend maturities in order to reduce the risk of falling interest rates must accept that they have increased their exposure to risk of unexpected inflation and have also increased the correlation of their fixed-income portfolio to their equity holdings. For them this might be a prudent trade-off. Note that investors who are willing to accept greater term risk should build a portfolio of individual bonds the maturities of which are tailored to meet their required cash flow need. And to reiterate, only bonds of the highest investment grade should be considered for purchase. Thus the choice of the prudent strategy is dependent on the unique financial needs of each investor, as well as on the risks about which he or she is most concerned.

Liquidity Risk and Reward

Although the two-factor model explains almost all of the risks and returns of a fixed-income portfolio, there is an additional risk factor that investors should consider besides credit and maturity. The third factor is liquidity.

The more liquid an investment, the lower will be the costs related to trading the security. Bid-offer spreads are negatively correlated with liquidity—the more liquid the security, the narrower will be the spread between the bid and the offer. In addition, other trading costs such as transaction fees, market impact costs, and dealer markups will tend to be less as liquidity improves. Thus investors prefer liquid to illiquid investments, all else being equal. The result is that investors require less liquid investments to provide higher yields. However, investors who are highly certain that they will be able to hold a security they purchase until maturity may not have much, if any, concern about the issue of liquidity. For these investors, at least for some portion of their portfolios, holding issues with a liquidity premium can be a prudent decision.

In chapter 3 we discussed the difference between "on-the-run" (newest issue) and "off-the-run" (older issue) securities. The newer security is more liquid and thus investors (or at least traders) are willing to pay a somewhat higher price (accept a somewhat lower yield). For buy-and-hold investors the higher yield of the older security might be considered a free stop at the dessert tray (especially since its maturity is also a bit shorter, making it a bit less susceptible to changes in interest rates). Another example will help illustrate the point.

The state of Missouri, a AAA credit, announces a new issue of $500 million of ten-year bonds yielding 4 percent. Given the size of the issue, and the quality of the credit, the issue will be very liquid (at least relative to other municipal bond issues). Now consider an issue with the same exact credit and term risks—a $10 million, fifteen-year State of Missouri general obligation bond that was issued five years ago, and thus has ten years left until maturity. That bond may not even have traded at all in the last several months. That bond will trade in the secondary market to yield a bit more than would the new primary issue. Perhaps the yield would be 4.1 percent, or even a bit higher. Investors who are virtually certain that they will be able to hold to maturity are likely to find the higher-yielding asset to be very attractive. Thus investors who have access to prices that are at or near the wholesale (interdealer) price will often find the secondary market to be a more attractive alternative than the primary market.

We have now completed our review of the efficient market hypothesis and its implications for fixed-income investors. We have also reviewed the risks and rewards of fixed-income investing. We are now ready to discuss the various alternative instruments and vehicles that investors can choose from when building a fixed-income portfolio. We will discuss the nature of each of the alternatives and evaluate the pros and cons of each. Chapters 5 through 9 cover the world of taxable investments. Chapter 10 covers the world of municipal securities.

CHAPTER FIVE

◆

The Securities of the U.S. Treasury, Government Agencies, and Government-Sponsored Enterprises

The greatest advantage from gambling comes from not playing at all.
> —Girolamo Cardano, sixteenth-century physician, mathematician, and quintessential Renaissance man

From a credit perspective U.S. Treasury securities are the safest instruments for U.S. fixed-income investors. They also have many other features that make them attractive investments. We, therefore, begin our journey through the taxable fixed-income world with the instruments that represent the direct debt obligations of the U.S. government.

U.S. Treasury Securities

The market for Treasury securities is the most liquid one in the world. The advantage this provides is that liquid markets result in trading costs that are typically very low, even for individual investors. The difference between the bid and the offer price on Treasury securities is extremely small—typically only about two thirty-seconds (by convention Treasury instruments trade in increments of 1/32 of a percent of face value or $31.25 for every $100,000 of face value). Another reason for trading costs being low for retail investors is that pricing is very transparent. As we discussed in the prior chapter, the lack of transparency in the pricing of municipal bonds allows brokers to exploit investors by adding large markups. However, as is the case with stocks, the prices of Treasury securities can be found in the *Wall Street Journal,* in other financial publications, or even on the Internet. Investors thus can easily monitor the amount of markup and commissions that are being charged if they purchase or sell a Treasury instrument through a brokerage firm.

Another advantage of owning Treasury instruments is that the interest earned, while taxable at the federal level, is not subject to state and local taxes. While corporate debt of the same maturity will carry a higher interest rate (reflecting credit risk), part of the higher rate reflects the difference in tax treatment. Taxable investors need to make sure they are making an apples-to-apples comparison, comparing after-tax yields, not pretax yields. This can be an important consideration for investors in high-tax states like California and New York. For investors in tax-deferred or tax-exempt accounts the yield premium on corporate bonds that is related to the difference in tax treatment comes without incremental risk. Of course, the incremental yield that is related to credit risk is compensation for risk.

A third advantage is that while most corporate and municipal bonds have call features, almost all Treasury securities do not. Thus investors in Treasury securities do not have to be concerned about reinvestment risk that results when interest rates fall and corporate and municipal issuers take advantage of the call feature. Of course, investors are compensated for the call risk with higher yields. For some investors that risk is worth considering in return for the higher yield. For others, taking that risk might be imprudent. Investors can diversify the risk of calls by owning some callable bonds and some noncallable bonds. As is always the case, there is no one right answer—just one that is right for each person. For a further discussion on this issue see Appendix A.

A fourth advantage Treasuries offer is that individuals can purchase them directly from the government, through the Treasury-Direct program. Participation in this program allows investors to avoid commissions and other transaction-related fees. While you can participate in this program via the telephone or even the mail, the process is made even easier if you have access to the Internet. The Web site is www.publicdebt.treas.gov. There you can open an account and participate in the regular periodic auctions at which new bonds are sold. The Web site provides the schedule of auctions. All you need is an account name, address, social security number, and an account at a financial institution to which payments of principal and interest can be made. While the program is designed for buy-and-hold investors, if you need to sell securities prior to maturity TreasuryDirect can handle that as well through what is called the Sell Direct service. Note that this service is only available for taxable accounts.

There is another significant feature of Treasury debt. Because of their risk-free nature (from a credit perspective), the yield on a Treasury instrument provides a benchmark against which other instruments can be compared. Before even considering purchasing any other type of instrument, investors should compare the yield on that instrument to the yield on a Treasury instrument of similar maturity. Investors can then determine if the incremental yield is sufficient to compensate them for the incremental risk. To the surprise of many investors Treasuries have often provided higher returns than riskier investments, despite their lower yield. The tax advantage mentioned earlier is one reason. Another is that the lack of a call feature results in superior returns whenever interest rates fall. Another reason is that sometimes the risk of default shows up, and the higher yield is not sufficient compensation. In addition, during a financial crisis, what is called a "flight to quality" occurs—principal protection becomes the main motivation of investors. As the safest and most liquid investments in the world, the prices of Treasury securities benefit from flights to quality. And finally, the lack of need for diversification (there is no credit risk) lowers costs. Unless you value the convenience of a mutual fund (e.g., automatic reinvestment of interest, ability to purchase in small increments) you can avoid the fees that a fund charges.

Bills, Notes, and Bonds

The U.S. government issues debt in three forms—bills, notes, and bonds. Treasury bills have maturities of a maximum of six months. They are issued with maturities of thirteen and twenty-six weeks. (The Treasury no longer issues one-year bills, though they could be brought back in the future.) Bills are the safest instruments because they not only entail no credit risk, but—because of their short maturity—they also entail little to no price risk.

Treasury instruments with an initial maturity of two to ten years are called notes. If the initial maturity of a Treasury instrument is beyond ten years it is called a bond.

There is a fourth type of Treasury security called a zero-coupon bond (or zero, for short). The term "zero" is used because the bonds pay no interest. Zeros are sold at a discount, and the interest comes in the form of price appreciation over time toward par (100). The price appreciation can be thought of as "imputed" or "phantom" interest. The difference between the discounted price paid and par determines the yield-to-maturity that will be earned. Zero-coupon bonds are also known as STRIPS (Separate Trading of Registered Interest and Principal of Securities). STRIPS are created by the secondary market by "stripping" away the interest and principal payments from the underlying bond to create both an interest-only bond and a principal-only bond (the zero-coupon bond). These instruments are then sold separately to investors.

The benefit of a zero-coupon bond is that it eliminates the reinvestment risk related to interest payments that are received by other bondholders—the phantom interest payments are in effect reinvested at the yield-to-maturity of the zero. A negative aspect of zeros is that the lack of interest payments results in the bond having a longer duration than an interest-bearing bond of similar maturity. In fact, the duration of a zero-coupon bond equals its maturity. Thus the price risk (volatility) of the zero is greater—and the longer the maturity, the greater the volatility. Another negative is that the market for zeros is not as liquid for retail investors, thus only buy-and-hold investors should even consider them.

In 1997 the Treasury began offering a new type of security that should be of interest to most investors, especially those concerned about the risk of unexpected inflation and the damage it can do to their portfolios and lifestyles. The instrument is called an inflation-protected security. There are two types of inflation-protected securities, TIPS and I bonds.

Treasury Inflation-Protected Securities

A TIPS is a bond, sold at auction, that receives a fixed stated rate of return but also increases its principal according to the changes in inflation, as measured by the nonseasonally adjusted U.S. City Average, All Items, Consumer Price Index for All Urban Consumers (CPI-U), published by the Bureau of Labor Statistics. Its fixed interest payment is calculated on the inflated principal, which is eventually repaid at maturity. For example, if a $1,000 TIPS had a stated (real) interest rate of 4 percent and the CPI rose 2 percent during the year, the math would work as follows. First, the adjustment to principal is calculated. Thus the principal would rise from $1,000 to $1,020 (an increase of 2 percent). Second, the real return would be calculated from the new principal. With a real rate of 4 percent, based on principal of $1,020, the amount of interest would be $40.80. This increase gives an investor protection against inflation by providing a guaranteed *real* return over a predetermined investment horizon. Interest is paid (the real rate) and accrued (the inflation adjustment) semiannually. At maturity the bondholder will receive the greater of the inflation-adjusted value or par. A further benefit of TIPS is that, like all Treasury debt, they are exempt from state and local taxes.

There is another significant benefit of TIPS. As we saw earlier in this section, the longer the term of a fixed-income asset, the higher the correlation of returns to equities. And we seek to have low correlation of fixed-income assets to equities in order to minimize portfolio risk. Because academic evidence has found that equities actually have a slightly negative correlation with inflation (inflation has a negative impact on equity returns as it increases business risk), TIPS should logically have a negative correlation with equities (because they should be highly correlated to inflation). This negative correlation helps reduce the overall risk of the portfolio. This is a distinct advantage over intermediate- to longer-term bonds.

Investors should note that TIPS, like most fixed-income instruments with a long maturity, are subject to price risk. For example, if an investor purchased TIPS when they had a 3 percent real interest rate, and the current real rate had risen to 4 percent, the principal value of TIPS would have fallen. A good example is the following. In April of 1999 the thirty-year TIPS (maturity 2029) was trading at par (100) and yielding 3.9 percent. By January 2000 the real yield had risen to 4.4 percent. This caused the price of the 2029 TIPS to fall from 100 to 92. Of course, the reverse is true. Using the same example, by March 2000 the real yield on the 2029 TIPS had fallen back to almost 4 percent, and the price of the TIPS had risen to about 97. Note, however, that TIPS with the same maturity as Treasury bonds should have less interest-rate risk because *real* interest rates are less volatile than *nominal* interest rates.

The volatility associated with TIPS may result in their not being the appropriate instrument for either investors with short investment horizons (not able to hold to maturity) or investors not willing to accept some interim price risk. Another negative is that an investor must pay the tax on both the real and the "unrealized" income (the amount of each year's inflated principal). This may have negative implications in terms of cash flow.

The following is a summary of the pros and cons investors should consider regarding TIPS.

Pros

- TIPS offer almost complete protection against unexpected inflation—they are the best pure inflation hedge. The reason that they don't offer complete protection is that TIPS are still subject to price risk (the real rate can change).

- TIPS should outperform conventional Treasuries when realized inflation is greater than expected inflation *plus* the risk premium. Note that the expected return of a TIPS should be slightly less than the expected return of a conventional U.S. Treasury security of the same maturity because investors in conventional Treasuries should receive a risk premium for bearing inflation risk. For example, the yield on a Treasury bond with ten years left to maturity might be 4 percent and the real yield on a TIPS with the same remaining term-to-maturity might be 2 percent. The difference between 4 and 2 percent reflects *both* the market's expectation of inflation for the period and a risk premium. While we currently have no way of separating the two, the inflation expectation might be 1.75 percent and the risk premium might be 0.25 percent.

- TIPS should also prove to be beneficial to investors who have above-average exposure to the risks of inflation (e.g., retirees).

- TIPS have negative correlation with equities and relatively low correlation with most types of fixed-income investments. Therefore, TIPS are great equity *and* fixed-income diversification agents.

- TIPS entail no credit risk.

- TIPS provide a *guaranteed* long-term real rate of return while diversifying the risk of equities in much the same way that short-term, high-quality fixed-income does.

- TIPS have lower expected volatility than conventional Treasury bonds of the same maturity due to lower sensitivity to nominal interest rate movements.

- TIPS have lower volatility than other investments that hedge unexpected inflation (e.g., commodities, real estate investment trusts).

- In case of deflation, TIPS investors are guaranteed the greater of the inflation-adjusted principal or par. This provides some protection against deflation if TIPS are not purchased above par.

- As is the case with all Treasury instruments, TIPS are exempt from state and local taxes.

Cons

- TIPS value could fluctuate significantly over short intervals. Investors who plan to hold to maturity, however, should not be affected by short-term price volatility.

- As stated above, the expected return of a TIPS should be slightly less than the expected return of a conventional U.S. Treasury security of the same maturity.

- TIPS would be expected to underperform conventional bonds when realized inflation is less than expected inflation.

- TIPS would not perform as well as intermediate- or long-term conventional bonds during periods of deflation.

- The inflation adjustment to principal is taxed. Therefore, unless an investor is not subject to income taxes, TIPS are not a *perfect* hedge against inflation.

- The deferral until maturity of the payment for the inflation adjustment may have negative cash flow implications—especially for those already in retirement.

I Bonds

The other inflation-protected Treasury security is an I bond. An I bond works like a TIPS in that it provides a fixed real rate of return and an inflation-protection component. There are, however, significant differences. The fixed rate on an I bond is announced by the Treasury in May and November and applies to all I bonds issued during the following six months. Like zero-coupon bonds their total return (fixed rate plus inflation adjustment) accrues in value. I bonds increase in value on the first of each month, and compound semiannually. They pay interest for up to thirty years. They can be bought and redeemed at most financial institutions. The redemption value can never go below par. All income is deferred for tax purposes until funds are withdrawn from the account holding the bond. The tax deferral feature makes an I bond a more attractive candidate than a TIPS for a taxable account. A further benefit of I bonds is that they are exempt from state and local taxes. Note that I bonds can only be held in taxable accounts.

Because they qualify for the "Education Bond Program," I bonds may provide a significant benefit. This program allows interest to be completely or partially excluded from federal income tax when the bond holder pays qualified higher education expenses at an eligible institution or state tuition plan in the same calendar year the bonds are redeemed. For 2003, the tax exclusion for single taxpayers begins to be reduced with a $58,500 modified adjusted gross income, and is eliminated for adjusted gross incomes of $73,500 and above. For married taxpayers filing jointly, the tax exclusion begins to be reduced with $87,750 of modified adjusted gross income, and is eliminated for modified adjusted gross incomes of $117,750 and above. Married couples must file jointly to be eligible for the exclusion.

The maximum amount of I bonds that can be purchased annually is $60,000 per individual, or $120,000 per couple. They can be bought in denominations of $50, $75, $100, $200, $500, $1000, and $10,000.

You can cash Series I bonds with issue dates of January 2003 and earlier any time after six months. Bonds with issue dates of February 2003 and after can be cashed anytime after twelve months. When you cash the bonds, you will receive the original investment plus the earnings. However, there is a prepayment penalty of three months interest if not held for a minimum of five years.

Note that I bonds act very much like TIPS. However, because they can be redeemed at par at any time, and thus have no volatility, they carry a lower real yield than do TIPS.

Alternatives to TIPS and I Bonds

For investors with either short investment horizons or a concern for stability of value prior to maturity, the preferred alternative to inflation-protected securities is a short-term fixed-income investment vehicle. Keep in mind that while traditional short-term fixed-income vehicles do not contain a specific inflation-protection component, their short-term nature offers similar protection. If the rate of inflation rises, interest rates will rise, and the short maturity structure will allow these vehicles to quickly capture the new higher rates. This is not true of long-term bonds. The other important characteristic of short-term investment vehicles is their highly stable value.

Investors considering inflation-protected securities should evaluate the decision on which is the preferred vehicle based on current yields, their current tax situation, their ability to hold to maturity, their ability to accept price risk, and whether the investment is for their taxable or tax-deferred account. These investments should be compared to the yields on alternative short-term fixed-income choices as well.

Given the positive attributes of inflation-protected securities there is another issue for investors to consider: How does an investor decide on an allocation between nominal-return bonds and real-return (inflation-protected) bonds? For the answer to that question see Appendix B.

Before moving beyond the world of Treasury instruments there is one other type of Treasury bond that investors should consider, an EE bond.

EE Bonds

EE bonds are another investment alternative with some attractive characteristics.

- They are obligations of the U.S. government and thus entail no credit risk.

- While they have a maturity of thirty years, the interest earned is based on the yield on the five-year Treasury note. Rates are announced each May and November with the yield set at 90 percent of the average yields on five-year Treasury securities for the preceding six months. That becomes the annual rate that applies to bonds for the next six-month earning period.

- EE bonds increase in value every month. Interest is compounded semiannually.

- As with all U.S. government obligations, interest earned on Series EE bonds is exempt from state and local income taxes. In addition, you can defer federal income tax until the bonds are redeemed (they stop earning interest after thirty years). The deferral feature provides a clear benefit. In addition, it also provides a potential benefit of being able to plan ahead and choose the best time to realize income for tax purposes (perhaps after retirement when the marginal tax bracket might be lower).

- Subject to an income limitation, there is also a special tax benefit available for education savings. For those that qualify, all or part of the interest earned on EE bonds can be excluded from taxable income when the bonds are redeemed to pay for postsecondary tuition and fees. The full interest exclusion is only available to taxpayers with modified adjusted gross income (which includes the interest earned) under a certain limit. These income limits apply in the year you use bonds for educational purposes—not the year you buy the bonds.

- EE bonds are highly liquid instruments. Newly issued EE bonds can be cashed in at any time after the mandatory one-year holding period. However, a three-month interest penalty will apply to bonds cashed before five years have elapsed. For example, if you buy a bond in May 2004 and cash it twenty-four months later, in May 2006, you get your original investment back plus twenty-one months of interest.

- Despite their thirty-year maturity, EE bonds are completely stable in value. At any time after one year they can be redeemed at par (thus there is no risk of loss of principal), less any penalty for early withdrawal. In addition, the penalty for early redemption is only the loss of three months of interest. Thus investors receive the benefit of the yield calculated as 90 percent of the five-year Treasury, without taking the price risk inherent in an instrument of that maturity. The limited price risk also results in a lower correlation with equities.

- EE Bonds can even be purchased directly from the Treasury in any amount of $25 or greater, and the purchase can be made via electronic debit from your checking or savings account. If purchased from a bank or savings and loan, EE bonds are sold at half their face value and are available in denominations ranging from $50 through $10,000. The Treasury Department guarantees that *new* issues of Series EE Bonds will double in value by twenty years from the issue date. In the event that rates are so low that a bond doesn't double in value over that time frame, the Treasury will make a one-time adjustment to double the value at that time. Thus another attractive feature of EE bonds is that they provide investors some protection against falling interest rates.

Besides the penalty for early redemption and the one-year minimum required holding period there is one other negative feature. The purchase of EE bonds is limited to a maximum issue price of $60,000 per social security number per annum ($120,000 per married couple). Investors can purchase up to $30,000 (issue price) in paper EE bonds per calendar year, and up to another $30,000 (issue price) in electronic EE bonds through the TreasuryDirect program.

EE bonds can only be held in taxable accounts. Therefore, even though they have some attractive characteristics, generally only investors in the lowest tax brackets will find them attractive (keeping in mind the aforementioned special tax benefit available for education savings). For higher-bracket investors, tax-exempt municipal bonds will generally be the preferred choice. There is one group of investors for whom EE bonds appear to be highly attractive. Dependent children under the age of 14 can currently earn up to $1,500 per year and have the income taxed at their (generally low-tax-bracket) tax rate.

We have completed our review of the securities of the U.S. Treasury. The next section deals with the securities of government agencies, federally related agencies, and government sponsored enterprises (GSEs). These instruments carry the highest AAA credit ratings. However, because they do not have the backing of the full faith and credit of the U.S. government they are not as impeccable credits as direct Treasury obligations. The exception are the securities of Ginnie Mae—they are backed by the full faith and credit of the U.S. government.

U.S. Government-Agency and -Sponsored Enterprise Securities

Since the 1930s the federal government has created both agencies and government-sponsored enterprises (GSEs) that have been designed to support specific sectors of the economy by reducing their cost of capital. In order to accomplish their objectives, these entities have been authorized to issue marketable securities. There are currently three U.S. government agencies, the Federal Home Loan Banks, the Federal Farm Credit Banks, and the Tennessee Valley Authority (TVA), and two GSEs, the Federal National Mortgage Association (Fannie Mae) and the Federal Home Loan Mortgage Corporation (Freddie Mac) that issue securities that should be of great interest to investors. (There are two other government agencies that sell securities primarily to institutional investors: the Overseas Private Investor Corporation [OPIC] and the Private Export Funding Corporation [PEFCO].)

With the exception of securities like Treasuries that carry the full faith and credit of the U.S. government, no other securities are considered safer than those of the agencies and the GSEs. All of their debt securities are rated AAA by the rating agencies. In addition, while none of them carry the backing of the full faith and credit of the U.S. government, the market considers them to have its *implied* support.

There are several reasons for the market's belief that these securities have the implied support of the U.S. government. The first is that the agencies and GSEs are creations of Congress and continue to enjoy tremendous political support. The second reason is that most of them have significant discretionary lines of credit with the U.S. Treasury. The third reason is that they are viewed as "too big to fail." Should one of these giants fail, the damage to the confidence in the U.S. economic system and markets in general would be so great that it could not be allowed to happen. The bottom line is that while they do not carry the full faith and credit of the U.S. government, the market believes that it is highly unlikely that the federal government would allow any of these securities to default. The lack of the support of the full faith and credit of the U.S. government, however, does result in investors demanding a slightly higher yield. In addition, while the markets for their securities are highly liquid, they are not as liquid as the market for Treasuries. The lower level of liquidity results in somewhat higher trading costs (bid-offer spreads are wider). Thus the market demands a small liquidity premium. The higher yields, but still exceptionally high credit ratings, make these securities attractive alternatives for individual investors. Another benefit is that the interest on the securities of the three agencies is generally exempt from state and local taxes. This is not the case, however, for the securities of the two GSEs.

For taxable investors, the yield premium over Treasuries that GSE securities provide may on occasion be more than offset by the lack of exemption from state and local taxes. This will be especially true in high-tax states such as New York and California. This is not an issue for tax-exempt or tax-deferred accounts, or for states without income taxes.

Another positive feature of agency and GSE securities is the relative transparency of pricing. For example, the *Wall Street*

Journal contains a section each day entitled "Government Agency & Similar Issues." The table contains the bid and offer prices of various securities of Fannie Mae, Freddie Mac, the Federal Farm Credit Bank, the Federal Home Loan Bank, and the TVA, as well as the prices of the mortgage-backed securities of the Government Mortgage Association (Ginnie Mae).

Role in a Portfolio

Because of their exceptional credit quality these instruments are appropriate for investors to consider, along with Treasury securities, as a core component of a fixed-income portfolio. This is especially true of buy-and-hold investors. The reason is that the liquidity premium they carry becomes a free lunch if there is no trading. In addition, the yield premium that taxable investors require on GSE securities (because interest is not exempt from state and local taxes as are Treasuries and agency securities) becomes a free lunch for tax-exempt and tax-deferred investors.

There are also structural reasons why agency and GSE securities may be very attractive. The first is that in a normally upward sloping yield curve, the longer the maturity, the larger will be the yield premium (spread) above Treasury securities. Thus investors who have the ability, willingness, or need to take risk may find that risk premium attractive. The second reason is that agency and GSE securities will often have a call feature. In return for accepting the risk of the call feature investors receive a higher coupon. For investors who have the ability, willingness, or need to take risk, buying securities with a call premium is a far more prudent way to attempt to earn higher returns than by taking credit risk—buying high-yield bonds. (See Appendix A for a discussion of callable bonds.) When it comes to taking credit risk, investors would be well served to remember the adage: "It takes an awful lot of interest to make up for unpaid principal."

One last word of caution: Prudent investors know to never treat the highly unlikely as impossible. For example, the Chicago area experienced two hundred-year floods within a ten-month period in 1986–87.[1] An example from the investment world is that the market currently perceives that the GSEs have the "moral support" of the U.S. government. This may not always be the case. Thus while these securities are of almost impeccable credit quality, and a default is extremely unlikely, it is not impossible. Thus investors should, at the very least, consider diversifying their fixed-income portfolios across the different agencies and GSEs (and other AAA-rated securities), and also consider owning some Treasury securities as well. Investors might consider a limit of 25 to 33 percent of their fixed-income allocation as the maximum that could be invested with any one agency or GSE. However, even this figure could be stretched if the maturity was relatively short. Remember, credit risk increases over time.

We have now completed our review of the world of securities related to the U.S. government, its agencies, and the GSEs. We will now cover the world of short-term fixed-income investments.

CHAPTER SIX

◆

The World of Short-Term Fixed-Income Securities

*There are two times in a man's life when he should not spec-
ulate: when he can't afford it, and when he can.*
——Mark Twain, *Following the Equator*

The distinction between saving (the goal of which is the preservation of capital) and investing (the goal of which is the creation of capital) is a crucial issue for investors to understand. Savings, because of low risk, and therefore low return, should be accumulated to meet emergency needs, cash flow needs, and short-term spending requirements (e.g., college tuition, purchase of a home or car). Once you have created this safety net, the balance of your capital should be invested.

In this chapter we will focus on fixed-income alternatives that are much more akin to savings than they are to investing. We begin with securities known as commercial paper.

Commercial Paper

Commercial paper consists of short-term, unsecured promissory notes issued primarily by corporations. The market is huge, with well over $1 trillion outstanding. Corporations issue commercial paper for two reasons—it is generally cheaper than bank loans and it diversifies their sources of funding. Most commercial paper is issued at a discount, paying par at maturity (a small part is interest bearing and pays interest and principal at maturity).

Maturities on commercial paper are usually no longer than 270 days. The reason is that commercial paper is exempt from the expensive SEC registration requirements of the Securities Act of 1933 as long as the maturity is less than 270 days. The maturity of most commercial paper is, however, much shorter—typically from one day to two months. The reason that the average maturity is so short is that in order for a bank (one of the major buyers of commercial paper) to borrow at the Federal Reserve's discount window it must put up what is called eligible collateral. In order for collateral to be eligible, its maturity cannot exceed fifty days. Because of the demand for eligible collateral, commercial paper trades at a lower yield—which is why corporations issue so much very short-term commercial paper.

Credit Quality

Just as is the case with corporate bonds, commercial paper carries a credit rating from agencies such as Moody's and Standard & Poor's. At one time only companies with very high credit ratings were able to issue commercial paper. However, this has changed. Companies with lesser credit quality have been able to issue paper by enhancing their own rating with some type of credit support. The support can be in the form of a letter of credit from a highly rated company (typically a financial institution or insurance company), or it can be in the form of collateralization with high-quality assets (e.g., accounts receivable, mortgage-backed securities). For the most part, commercial paper is a very safe investment because the financial situation of a company can easily be predicted over a few months. As a result there have only been a handful of cases where corporations have defaulted on their commercial paper. But caution should still apply. Thus, a good rule of thumb is that you should only consider paper with the highest rating of A1 (S&P rating) or P1 (Moody's rating).

Buying and Selling

Commercial paper is issued in one of two ways. The traditional route has been through broker-dealers. However, some corporations have such large programs that they now issue paper themselves directly to the investing public.

While there are some issuers that sell commercial paper in denominations of $25,000, it is usually issued in denominations of $100,000 or more. Thus only high-net-worth individuals can even consider this market. Despite the size of the primary market for commercial paper there is very little secondary trading. While a dealer, or the issuer in the case of directly placed commercial paper, will generally repurchase the paper if the need arises, individual investors should only purchase the paper if they plan to buy and hold.

Yields

Yields on commercial paper are somewhat higher than they are on Treasury bills. The higher yield results from three factors. First is the increased credit risk. Second is the lower level of liquidity. The liquidity premium, however, is very small because of the very-short-term nature of the paper, and most buyers plan to hold to maturity. And third is the taxing of interest on commercial paper at the state and local level, while this is not true for Treasuries. These are factors that should be considered in evaluating the investment decision. Investors can track the yields on commercial paper very easily. The *Wall Street Journal* reports on them daily, as does the Federal Reserve at their Web site—federalreserve.gov/releases/cp.

The bottom line is that for high-net-worth individuals, commercial paper can be an attractive alternative, providing an incremental return over Treasury bills. And while investors have incurred very few losses over the past several decades, the basic principle of prudent investing still applies: Don't put too many eggs in one basket. Thus if your portfolio is not large enough to allow you to diversify across issuers, the best way to access this market is through money-market funds—the next investment vehicle we will discuss.

Money-Market Funds

A money-market fund is an open-end mutual fund that invests only in short-term debt obligations. By SEC regulation such a fund must have a highly diversified portfolio that is composed of the securities of creditworthy corporations, banks, and other financial institutions and federal, state, and local governments. By law, the average maturity of the fund cannot exceed ninety days, though the term of any one instrument can be as long as 397 days. Thus a money-market fund involves almost no interest rate risk. The generally high credit quality of its investments, and the payment of interest on a monthly basis, allows it to maintain a net asset value (NAV) of $1.

There are two distinct categories of money-market funds—taxable and tax-exempt.

Taxable Money-Market Funds

Within the category of taxable money-market funds there are three types, general, U.S. government, and Treasury-only. U.S. Treasury funds invest only in direct U.S. Treasury obligations, and thus entail no credit risk. In addition, interest is exempt from state and local taxes. U.S. government funds hold obligations of the U.S. Treasury as well as those of the agencies of the U.S. government. As we have discussed, while agency debt is rated AAA, it does not have the backing of the full faith and credit of the government (only the market's perception of an implied guarantee). The lack of the backing of the full faith and credit of the government makes agency bonds not as an impeccable a credit as Treasury debt. Agency debt thus carries slightly higher interest rates. The interest on the debt of two of the agencies, the Federal Home Loan Bank and the Federal Farm Credit Bank System, is also exempt from state and local taxes.

The third type of taxable money-market fund is a general fund. It invests in U.S government debt as well as in the short-term debt of large, high-quality corporations and banks in order to try to achieve higher returns.

Tax-Exempt or Municipal Money-Market Funds

The second category of money-market funds is known as tax-exempt or municipal money-market funds. They invest in the short-term securities of state and local government agencies, and provide interest income that is tax-free (subject to the limitations imposed by the alternative minimum tax rules, or AMT). There are two types of tax-exempt funds. National tax-exempt funds invest in municipal obligations issued by state and local governments across the country. Such funds provide income that is free of federal income taxes. Most states, however, only provide a tax exemption for interest earned on debt obligations of their own state. Therefore, most of the interest from national tax-exempt funds is generally taxable at the state and local level. This creates the need for single-state funds that only purchase the municipal obligations of a single state. Depending on the state tax rate, a national or single-state fund will be the preferred choice.

Taxable or Tax-Exempt?

While the appeal of the tax exemption is high, sometimes the mathematics show that a taxable fund will actually provide higher after-tax returns. To determine which alternative is best, you need to calculate the tax equivalent yield (TEY) of a municipal money-market fund. As we discussed in chapter 1 the TEY is (approximately) equal to the tax-exempt yield divided by 100 percent minus your tax rate.

$$TEY = Y / (100\% - \text{tax rate})$$

When doing the math, remember that you also need to consider that interest on Treasury and federal agency debt is exempt from state taxes, while interest on nonlocal municipal debt may be taxable. The potential for the AMT to play a role should also be considered.

Role in a Portfolio

The main goal of these funds is the preservation of principal, not high return. Thus money-market funds should be considered savings vehicles, not investments. If return is the goal, there are better alternatives. As we saw in the first chapter, investors have generally been well rewarded for extending term risk beyond the average term of a money-market fund. Short-to-intermediate-term bonds (or bond funds) would be the preference if return were the main objective. Money-market funds should be used to hold funds needed for unanticipated expenses and as a "holding place" for funds that will be invested in the near future.

Most financial planners recommend that investors hold an amount equal to three to six months of living expenses in a money-market fund (or other very short-term fund with a similar high credit quality) for the proverbial rainy day. Given their role, investors should seek funds that invest only in the highest-investment-grade securities. With this restriction, and the limitation on maturity restricting the ability to take interest rate risk, funds should be chosen mainly on the basis of which has the lowest cost. The average money-market fund has expenses of about 0.6 percent, but some funds carry expenses as low as 0.15 percent. Convenience can also come into play. You might be willing to pay somewhat higher expenses for the convenience of check-writing privileges, and also for having all of your investments at one custodian. There are, however, funds with expense ratios well above one percent—and they should be avoided like the plague. That is simply too high a price to pay for any convenience benefit.

When looking at a fund's operating expense ratio, a word of caution is warranted—sometimes a fund will *temporarily* waive some of its expenses. Therefore, you should determine whether a fund is gaining its cost advantage by maintaining low expenses over time, or by temporarily waiving fees. This information can be obtained by reviewing the prospectus.

Risk of Loss

While money-market funds do not provide a guarantee against loss, thanks to the tight restrictions imposed by the SEC, their track record is almost unblemished. For competitive reasons most fund sponsors have maintained a policy of preventing their funds from "breaking the buck" (the NAV falling below $1). If a fund were allowed to break the buck, confidence in the fund would be shattered. There have been several instances where fund sponsors have had to subsidize the fund's value because of credit losses. High-expense funds might seek to keep their net yield competitive by investing in riskier securities—and sometimes losses will be incurred. In addition, the very low interest rate environment of 2003–04 forced companies to at least temporarily waive some of their fees, or the funds would have provided negative returns.

Summary

The convenience and safety of money-market funds have made them extremely popular vehicles. Given their role in the portfolio, investors should seek funds with both a track record of very low expenses and a history of investing only in the strongest credits.

Certificates of Deposit

A certificate of deposit (CD) is a short- or medium-term, interest-bearing, FDIC-insured debt instrument offered by banks and savings and loans. FDIC insurance is only provided on accounts of up to $100,000 per social security number, per bank. A CD has a stated interest rate and maturity date, and can be issued in any denomination.

Types of CDs

CDs can be either negotiable (marketable) or nonnegotiable. If a CD is nonnegotiable, money removed before maturity is subject to an early withdrawal penalty—and there are no strict guidelines governing the penalty that can be imposed.

CDs of over $100,000 are generally known as "jumbo CDs." Because of the economies of scale they provide the bank, they generally carry a slightly higher interest rate. Almost all jumbo CDs, as well as some small CDs, are negotiable. Many large brokerage firms now market CDs. They will also act as custodian, simplifying the paperwork. Some firms even provide marketability by standing ready to buy back CDs prior to maturity. There are also many Web sites that list current offerings, allowing investors to shop the market nationwide.

Banks have become very creative in the types of CDs that they offer. For example, CDs can be either fixed or floating (a variable CD). They can also have call or put (the investor has the right to early redemption) features. CDs can even have a "step-down" feature—the investor might be offered a higher initial rate but the rate is subject to downward revision should a benchmark (e.g., Treasury bill or Eurodollar) rate fall. They can also have a "step-up" feature. And they can even be tied to the performance of the stock market. While most of the offerings favor the banks (especially the ones tied to the performance of the stock market—those should almost certainly be avoided), at times the marketing departments of banks create products that favor the investor (probably because the marketing staffs, and possibly even the finance staffs, don't fully understand the risks). Thus while most of the time CDs may not provide the best investment choice, there are occasions when they are definitely worth considering—for example, if a bank offered a long-term CD with a put option, allowing the investor to redeem early should rates rise, but hold to maturity if they remain stable or fall. As is always the case, prudence dictates that you don't invest in anything where you don't fully understand the nature of the pricing and the risks.

There is another type of CD that we need to cover—dollar-denominated CDs issued by foreign banks. Dollar-denominated CDs issued by foreign banks abroad are known as Eurodollar CDs, or Euro CDs. CDs issued by U.S. branches of foreign banks are known as Yankee CDs. Euro and Yankee CDs need to provide a higher rate of interest because they lack FDIC insurance. The issuer is also able to offer a higher rate because it has lower reserve requirement costs (the Federal Reserve requires U.S. bank deposits to be backed by reserves). Since the issuer will earn less on the funds raised in the U.S. (because of the reserve requirements it cannot lend out the full amount) it has to offer a lower rate of interest on U.S. deposits than it can on Euro CDs. A third reason for their higher rate is the "sovereign" (country) risk the investor accepts. The size of the risk premium a Euro or Yankee CD will provide will depend on the credit rating of the bank, the specific sovereign risk perceived by the market, and the confidence in the global banking system in general. A fourth reason for the yield premium is their reduced liquidity (even if they are marketable).

Yield and Credit Risk

Yields on CDs are generally somewhat higher than they are on Treasury instruments. However, taxable investors must consider the exemption from state and local taxes that Treasuries enjoy and CDs do not. This is irrelevant for tax-exempt or tax-deferred accounts. Once the tax differential is considered, for taxable investors Treasuries might provide the higher after-tax rate of return. Investors should also consider that Treasuries have no credit risk, they are more marketable, and there are no prepayment penalties.

The yield on a bank CD is influenced by the credit rating of the bank, even when FDIC insurance applies. Before purchasing any CD, investors should determine the risk involved by checking the issuer's credit rating. There are several rating services, including Duff & Phelps, Fitch, Moody's, and Standard & Poor's. Credit risk is not much of an issue for amounts of $100,000 or less since FDIC insurance is available. For amounts greater than $100,000 diversification of credit risk becomes important, especially if a bank is not a highly rated one. Investors should note that while the FDIC does insure that no losses will occur, it does not guarantee the timely payment of interest and principal. If a bank fails, CD holders will eventually have their funds returned, but it may not be at maturity.

Summary

CDs (at least those that carry FDIC insurance) are generally safe investments and worth considering for a portion of a fixed-income portfolio, especially for tax-deferred or tax-exempt accounts.

Stable-Value Investment Vehicles

As we ended the first quarter of 2004, money market accounts, a traditional safe harbor for investors, were yielding less than 1 percent, the lowest level in decades. Even ten-year Treasury bonds were yielding less than 4 percent. If interest rates rose, longer-term bond prices would fall dramatically. Investors who are unwilling to, unable to, or have no need to take the risks of equity ownership search for vehicles that can provide higher than money-market yields without taking either significant credit or price and term risk. Stable-value investment vehicles (also called interest-income, principal-preservation, or guaranteed-interest funds) just might fit the bill. Well-designed vehicles can provide investors with higher yields without exposing them to significant credit or price risk.

Stable-value investments are fixed-income investment vehicles offered through defined-contribution savings plans and individual retirement accounts (IRAs). The assets in stable-value funds are generally very high quality bonds and insurance contracts, purchased directly from banks and insurance companies, that guarantee to maintain the value of the principal and all accumulated interest. They deliver safety and stability by preserving principal and accumulated earnings. In that respect, they are similar to money-market funds but offer higher returns.

Stable-value options in participant-directed defined-contribution plans allow participants access to their accounts at full value for withdrawals and transfers as permitted by the defined-contribution plan. However, since they are often purchased within retirement plans, the plan itself may have withdrawal restrictions (and the stable-value fund itself may impose other restrictions, which will be discussed below).

The higher returns offered by stable-value investments make them comparable to intermediate bonds without the volatility. In that respect they offer unique risk-return characteristics—perhaps explaining why they are included in two-thirds of employee-directed 401(k) and 403(b) plans, representing over 33 percent of assets that according to the Stable Value Investment Association total in excess of $300 billion in value (www.stablevalue.org). In order to gain an understanding of these vehicles we will look at the types of investments they make and how they are able to offer stability of value yet provide attractive returns.

Investment Portfolios

Until recently, most stable-value vehicles were structured as guaranteed investment contracts (GICs). These are contracts issued by financial institutions—typically a highly rated insurance company, though it could also be a bank—guaranteeing investors a fixed rate of return. In the 1980s, however, several insurers (Executive Life, Mutual Benefit Life, and Confederation Life), financed by high-yield bonds, sold GICs to retirement plans and then went under.

The result is that today most stable-value assets are structured as "synthetic GICs," also known as "wrapped bonds." Synthetic GICs are created by purchasing short-term to intermediate-term bonds, including U.S. government and agency bonds, mortgages, and asset-backed securities. The bonds purchased are generally of the highest investment grade ratings (AAA and AA). Some vehicles include a provision for a very limited allocation to lower-rated paper (e.g., 10 percent). In addition, provisions are often made for the portfolio to invest in futures, options, and forward currency contracts (see glossary). The portfolio is then protected from fluctuation in value by the purchase of insurance "wrappers." If the market value of a stable-value portfolio falls below the book value of the portfolio, the insurer pays the difference, keeping the fund's value *stable*. On the other hand, if the portfolio's market value exceeds its book value, the fund pays the insurer the difference. The wrapper allows the stable-value vehicle to fix its net asset value at, say, $10 a share (i.e., like a money-market fund). However, a stable-value fund is not a money-market fund and there can be no assurance that the fund will be able to maintain a stable value over time. Also note that if a fund holds derivative positions they can be more volatile and less liquid than traditional securities. The greater volatility of these instruments could lead to additional sources of market losses. Typically the wrapper will cost the vehicle from 15 to 25 basis points, depending on the credit quality of the portfolio, the structure of the wrapper and supply-demand conditions of the market for this type of portfolio insurance. Because of the insurance wrapper, the returns for the funds come solely from their yield. Thus there is no potential for capital gains, and very little risk of loss to consider (unless the credit rating of the insurer and the underlying instruments are not of the highest investment grades). Additionally, the stable-value vehicle may hold insurance company–issued GICs, or similar instruments, as well as cash equivalents.

Risks

Stable-value funds appear to be a good deal for investors, providing returns similar to those of high-grade intermediate-term bonds with the volatility of a money market account. However, while the risks are minimal, the investments are not risk-free. The earnings of stable-value vehicles can be outpaced by inflation, their yields typically lag the market, and unlike money-market funds that invest solely in U.S. government securities they are not entirely immune to a credit blowup among the issuers of the bonds they hold. Although the insurers put their financial weight behind stabilizing the fund's net asset value—"guaranteeing" that investors will never experience a loss in their invested capital— they do not shield the fund from credit problems. Although credit blowups do not impact the NAV, credit problems do result in lower future yields for a stable-value fund. In addition, investors accept the credit risk of the insurance provider. Thus it is important to analyze both the risk profile (credit rating, maturity, individual bond structure, and liquidity) of the individual securities held in the portfolio and the credit rating of the insurance providers. Many stable investment vehicles diversify (but do not eliminate) the credit risk of the insurance provider by purchasing contracts from several providers.

Costs

If the characteristics of stable-value funds are of interest to you, be sure to keep a particularly close eye on costs, as you should with any investment vehicle. Within defined-contribution plans such as 401(k)s and 403(b)s, such annual expenses average less than 0.5 percent, but in an IRA the fees are likely to be as high as 1.0 percent, according to the Stable Value Investment Association.

Restrictions

Most stable-value offerings place restrictions on when or how often you can withdraw cash from their funds. For example, they may limit the number of withdrawals that can be made during a specified time period. Consequently, they typically don't offer the same degree of liquidity, or ready access to one's cash, as do money-market funds. (Note that the liquidity restrictions allow them to invest in less liquid and higher-yielding investments.) In addition, some plans will force investors to move their withdrawal amount into an equity fund, instead of another fixed-income investment (preventing investors from shifting their stable-value assets into the bond market whenever it looks as though interest rates may decline or into money-market funds whenever it looks as though interest rates may rise). Also, if the investment vehicle is inside of a retirement plan it will be subject to the rules of that plan.

Why Are Returns So Stable?

Despite purchasing bonds that fluctuate in value, stable-value investment vehicles produce very stable returns. They are able to do so because of the insurance wrapper that they purchase. The insurance wrapper allows them to use "book value" accounting instead of market value accounting. Book value accounting means that the fund is valued based on what it paid for each contract, not on what each contract might be worth at any given time if it were sold on the open market. Book value accounting keeps the price of stable-value funds steady despite changes in the market value of the underlying securities. This makes it possible for the fund to pay interest rates similar to bonds, with minimal fluctuations in share prices.

Returns Change Slowly over Time

A stable-value investment vehicle contains a number of GICs and individual bonds. Each time a contract or bond matures, the principal sum is paid back to the fund and the fund must then reinvest it in a new contract or bond at whatever interest rate is prevailing at the time. If rates are going down, the current rate will be lower than the rate that was being earned previously, and the return to the stable-value fund will gradually decline. Similarly, if current rates are higher than the rate on the matured contract, the stable-value fund's return will gradually increase. Most stable-value managers ladder, or diversify, the maturities of the contracts held within the stable-value fund to smooth these changes. Because book value accounting returns are much more stable and the correlation of stable-value funds to equity holdings is lower than it is for bond funds, stable-value vehicles are excellent diversification tools for a portfolio.

Cash Flows Can Affect Returns

If large sums of money flow into a stable-value fund when interest rates are high, and small sums of money flow into a stable-value fund when interest rates are low, everyone in the fund enjoys higher than average returns because more money is invested in contracts that continue to pay high rates until their maturity date. The reverse is also true.

The timing of the cash flows is typically the main concern for the manager of the stable-value fund. Without the ability to accurately forecast contributions and withdrawals, managing the fund for stable value would become very difficult. In addition, the cost of the insurance wrappers would certainly increase (withdrawals would rise whenever interest rates increased and losses would be incurred). This is why stable-value funds are only available in tax-exempt or tax-deferred account environments with heavy withdrawal restrictions. The complete investment freedom of a taxable account environment has proven to be too great a hurdle for the economics to overcome.

Recommendation

Stable-value funds can be considered for a portion of one's fixed-income allocation. With that in mind, the following suggestions are offered:

- A significant amount of due diligence should be undertaken on the credit worthiness of both the underlying investments and any insurance contracts, as well as on any restrictions on withdrawals.

- The vehicle should carry contracts with multiple, high-quality insurers (insurers that carry at least a rating of AA, or the equivalent, from one of the major rating agencies).

- More than 90 percent of the portfolio should be covered with insurance contracts.

- At least 90 percent of the vehicle's assets should be in investment-grade bonds that are rated at least AA.

- The average maturity and duration of assets should be short-term (e.g., not longer than about three years). This helps ensure that the fund won't be stuck with longer-term low-yielding bonds if rates start to rise.

- If the portfolio utilizes derivatives, there should be a thorough understanding of their usage and whether any leverage is involved.

- The fund's management team should have a record of producing returns that are competitive with its stable-value peers or indices.

- Costs are critical. Therefore, consider only very low-cost vehicles, preferably with annual expenses under 0.5 percent.

An example of a stable-value product that should be considered is the TIAA Traditional Annuity, available in many 403(b) accounts and in the TIAA-CREF IRA. This product is backed by the claims-paying ability of TIAA, a very highly rated (AAA) insurance company. The product carries no sales or surrender charges.

We have now completed our review of the world of short-term fixed-income securities. The next category of fixed-income instruments that we will cover is corporate securities.

CHAPTER SEVEN

◆

The World of Corporate Fixed-Income Securities

If investors invest in a fashion that exceeds their own risk tolerance, so that when things go awry (as they inevitably will from time to time) they must abandon their strategy, they have done themselves a disservice by engaging in the strategy in the first place.

—Robert Arnott, president and
chief financial officer of First Quadrant

In this chapter we will cover various types of corporate fixed-income securities. We will begin with investment-grade corporate bonds. Before we do so, however, we point out that the securities of the two GSEs (discussed in chapter 5) are corporate bonds, as both Fannie Mae and Freddie Mac are public corporations. Thus most of the issues that we discussed that are related to the securities of the GSEs (e.g., credit risk, event risk, call risk) generally apply to corporate bonds as well. We will also cover the world of high-yield (junk) bonds, preferred stocks, and convertible bonds.

The market for corporate bonds can be divided into the two broad categories of investment grade and noninvestment grade. Investment-grade bonds are those that carry a Moody's rating of AAA, Aa, A, or Baa, or an S&P rating of AAA, AA, A, or BBB. Issues with ratings below these levels are speculative, and are categorized as high-yield bonds.

Investors also must be careful to check the rating of each individual security because they are independently rated. For example, just as General Motors has many different types of cars (e.g., Chevrolets, Pontiacs, Cadillacs) with unique characteristics, General Motors has also issued many different debt instruments, each with its own unique rating. The specific rating assigned to a security will depend on the terms contained in the indenture. Thus one issuer can have securities that trade with different credit ratings. Factors that impact the credit rating of a specific issue include whether the bond is collateralized (and the quality of the collateral), whether the bond is subordinated (other debt has preference in terms of repayment in the event of a default), the potential for event risk, and even its maturity.

Investors should also be aware that the ratings of corporate bonds can and do change frequently due to changes in the economic climate or to event risk appearing. An example of how changing economic conditions can impact asset values would be when oil prices fell in the mid-1980s from above $30 a barrel to about $10 a barrel. The prices of homes collapsed in many parts of the oil belt (i.e., Texas, Louisiana, Colorado, Oklahoma). They fell so sharply that many homeowners mailed in their keys to their mortgage lender. Similarly, in the pre-Microsoft days Seattle was basically a one-company town. Whenever the aircraft manufacturing industry, especially Boeing, got into serious trouble (as it did in the 1970s), the prices of homes in Seattle came under serious pressure. Other good examples of how events can lead to changes in credit ratings are Merck's downgrading from AAA to AA- due to the problems caused by the recall of its popular drug Vioxx and the downgrading of many bonds of the state of California in 2003 due to the state's fiscal problems.

Because ratings can change frequently they must constantly be monitored. In addition, as was discussed earlier, not all AAA bonds are created equal—corporate bonds are significantly riskier than municipal bonds of the same rating. Finally, the call provisions of corporate debt instruments can be far more complex than they are for municipal bonds. The bottom line is that corporate bonds are far trickier investments than Treasuries or municipal bonds. Investors need to tread carefully if they wish to invest in this sector of the market, especially if they are going to do so on their own.

The attraction of corporate bonds is the higher yield they provide over Treasuries. As we have discussed, part of the yield premium is a result of the exemption from state and local taxes that applies to the interest on Treasury debt, but not to corporate debt. This is a consideration for investments held in taxable accounts. The other factors are their greater exposure to economic risk and their lower level of liquidity (resulting in greater trading costs). And the lower the credit rating the greater the economic risks and the lower the level of liquidity.

The question for investors is the following: Given the role of fixed-income investing in a portfolio, is the higher yield sufficient to justify all of the risks? Given that a high (if not the highest) priority for investors, whether in the accumulation or withdrawal stage, is safety or stability of principal, the prudent choice is to restrict holdings to only the two highest investment grades, AAA and AA. One of the major reasons is that as the credit rating decreases, the correlation with equity returns increases. This is a strong negative feature of lower-rated bonds—they are more likely than higher-rated bonds to perform poorly at the same time that stocks are performing poorly. Another compelling reason is that the historical evidence (as presented in chapter 2) suggests that investors simply have not been sufficiently rewarded for taking incremental credit risk. The reasons are related not only to the credit losses incurred, but also to features (i.e., calls) that can negatively impact returns.

Lack of Transparency of Pricing

As we have discussed, transparency of pricing is a critical issue for investors. Transparency provides at least some protection against exploitation by Wall Street. Unfortunately, most corporate bonds are not even listed on the major exchanges, making it difficult to obtain true market pricing; investors are prevented from learning how much markup was added by the broker to the wholesale price. Even among listed bonds the financial press reports on the prices of very few issues. For example, the *Wall Street Journal* reports daily on the prices of just forty corporate bonds, and many of them are from the same few issuers. Given the lack of transparency, individual do-it-yourself investors considering purchasing corporate bonds should only buy new issues (which are all offered at the same price to every investor). In addition, they should only buy them if they intend to buy and hold them.

Need for Diversification

As we have discussed, diversification is one of the most important concepts of prudent investing. Because Treasury securities entail no credit risk, there is no need for diversification. However, as we move beyond Treasuries the need for diversification increases in direct relationship to the credit rating—the lower the rating, the greater the need. Since government agency and government-sponsored enterprise securities entail little credit risk, very little diversification is required. Investors might, for example, own some Treasury debt and also allocate some of their assets to each of the GSEs and agencies. Once we move to corporate debt the risks become much greater. Since it is not economical to buy or sell less than $50,000 per corporate bond, only investors with a fixed-income allocation of at least $500,000 should even consider buying individual corporate bonds. That would allow them to limit their exposure to any one issuer to a maximum of 10 percent of their fixed-income allocation. In addition, because of the relatively low level of liquidity in the corporate bond market, individuals acting on their own should only make purchases if the expectation is to buy and hold. Investors with less than $500,000 of fixed-income assets who are seeking to capture the incremental yield of corporate bonds should use either low-cost mutual funds, like those of Vanguard, or exchange-traded funds.

While we have discussed why prudent investors should consider purchasing only corporate bonds of the two highest grades, high-yield bonds have received so much attention that we need to discuss their attributes and why they are appropriate only for speculators, not investors.

High-Yield Bonds

Well-informed investors avoid the no-win consequences of high-yield fixed-income investing.
> —David Swensen, chief investment officer of the Yale endowment, *Unconventional Success*

As we have discussed, the riskier the credit of the issuer is perceived to be, the greater the risk premium, in the form of a higher interest rate, the market will require.

A study, "Explaining the Rate Spread on Corporate Bonds," sought the answers to the following questions:[1]

- How much of the spread between corporate and Treasury bonds is explained by expected losses from defaults? Some percentage of corporate bonds is likely to default. Defaults generally result in recovery rates well below 100 percent. Investors must be compensated for the expected losses. The riskier the credit (observed by the credit rating assigned by rating agencies such as Moody's and S&P) the greater the expected losses.

- How much of the spread is explained by the tax premium? Interest on U.S. government securities is not taxed at the state or local level while interest on corporate debt is taxed. Investors must be compensated for the tax differential.

- Is the incremental risk of corporate bonds diversifiable or systematic (nondiversifiable)?

The following is a summary of the study's conclusions regarding these questions:

- The difference in tax treatment and expected default losses do not explain the spread well. For example, the authors found that in the case of a ten-year A-rated corporate bond just 18 percent of the spread was explained by default risk while taxes accounted for 36 percent. There must be a risk premium demanded by investors that explains the remaining spread.

- The Fama-French three-factor model explains as much as 85 percent of the spread that is not explained by taxes and expected default loss. Again, the three factors are exposure to the risk factor of the overall stock market and to the risk factors of size and value. These are systematic risks that *cannot* be diversified away.

It is logical that compensation for risk changes over time as economic conditions change. If changes in the required risk premium affect both corporate bond and stock prices, corporate bonds contain risk that cannot be diversified away. The study found that such a relationship does exist—corporate bond returns were positively related to the equity market factor as well as the size and value factors. This is only logical: "If common equity receives a risk premium for this systematic risk, then corporate bonds must also earn a risk premium." Very importantly, the authors found that the longer the maturity and the lower the credit risk, the stronger the correlation is to the risk factors.

The findings of this study have significant implications for investors. We begin with an understanding that high-yield bonds are hybrid securities.

A Hybrid Security

High-yield bonds are often recommended to investors because of their greater yield and because they have a nonperfect correlation with both equities and U.S. government securities and the securities of corporate bonds with the highest credit ratings (AAA and AA). Investors considering, for example, a 60 percent equity and 40 percent fixed-income portfolio (based upon their risk tolerance) might be counseled to allocate one-fourth of their fixed-income holdings to high-yield debt (10 percent of the portfolio). A problem is created because high-yield debt is really a *hybrid* instrument; while it is called debt, as we have seen, it has equity-like risk characteristics. This is why it has nonperfect correlation with both equities and debt. Since high-yield debt is really taking on equity risk, the investor will actually be holding a portfolio that has more equity risk than a 60 percent–40 percent portfolio would hold. And as the results of the aforementioned study show, the lower the credit rating, and the longer the maturity of the debt, the more equity-like the high-yield security becomes.

The Role of High-Yield Bonds in the Portfolio

The main purpose of fixed-income securities for most investors is to provide stability to their portfolio, allowing them to take equity risk. While it is true that high-yield debt has nonperfect correlation with equities, the correlation may increase at just the wrong time—when the distress risk of equities shows up. Therefore, investors should always remember that correlations are not static values.

There are several other issues that impact the decision on whether or not high-yield securities should play a role in the portfolio. They include liquidity, asset location, and the distribution of returns.

Illiquid Securities

High-yield bonds are generally highly illiquid instruments (and the lower the credit rating, the more illiquid the instrument is likely to be). For example, a typical U.S. high-yield index includes about 1,500 securities, with only about 25 percent of them trading even at least once per month.[2] The less liquid an asset class, the greater will be trading costs, including not only bid-offer spreads, but market-impact costs as well. In addition, in times of crises the markets for illiquid assets can virtually dry up—buyers disappear and sales can only be made if the seller is willing to accept a severe discount. (It is like trying to sell a condominium apartment in a glutted market where prices are falling.) As a result, investors in high-yield bonds demand an incremental risk premium. Thus a liquidity premium must explain part of the differential in yields between high-yield bonds and Treasuries. Unfortunately, this liquidity risk rears its head in times of crisis, just when equity prices are under pressure, leading to high correlation with equity prices just when we need low correlation—again illustrating that correlations are not static values.

Other Negative Characteristics

Another negative feature of high-yield bonds is that they often have call provisions. Investors generally think of the call feature in terms of the risk that the bond will be called if interest rates fall. This is true for high-grade bonds. However, for lower-rated bonds, there is an additional risk created by the call feature. The risk is that the credit rating of the issue will improve sufficiently for the issuer to call the bond and issue a new bond with a higher rating, lowering interest costs. A similar risk is created by what is known as a "clawback" provision. Some high-yield securities allow the issuer to call a predetermined amount of the bond if the issuer is able to do an equity offering. The good news for investors in general is that the investment risk is reduced. That, however, doesn't do *you* any good if *your* bond is called.

There is another often overlooked issue related to illiquid assets—illiquidity *artificially* induces what is known as positive serial correlation (also known as autocorrelation) of returns. Serial correlation is the correlation of a variable with itself over successive time intervals. An example will clarify the issue.

Imagine that you have to sell your home in order to take a job in another town. How would you determine the price at which you should list your home? Typically you would look at the sale prices of similar properties. But what if no sales had occurred in the past year? And what if economic conditions had changed dramatically during that period? Would the last sales price be truly reflective of current valuations? Would those prices correctly reflect current valuations for the homes in your neighborhood? If you believed those prices were accurate, then you would be assuming that prices had been stable. Of course, both assumptions are likely to be incorrect.

The calculation of the value of an index (or the value of the assets in a portfolio) that prices bonds for which there has been no active market will include prices that are either outdated or are based on what is known as "matrix pricing." The latter is an attempt to estimate the market price by evaluating the prices of bonds that have *similar* risk characteristics but have traded more recently. If estimates are based on prices that are outdated, then the true price is probably different. Thus the price may be overstated or understated. Both outdated prices and matrix pricing tend to give the appearance of greater price stability than is actually being experienced (if the securities had actually traded). Thus illiquidity and the resulting autocorrelation leads to an underestimation of volatility and of the real risks of an asset class. The result is that for portfolios of illiquid securities, reported returns will tend to be smoother than true economic returns, understating volatility and overstating risk-adjusted performance measures such as the Sharpe ratio. The issue of serial correlation and its implication is important to keep in mind when considering any illiquid investment (e.g., emerging-market bonds, venture capital, hedge funds).

There is another risk-related issue that should be considered before investing in high-yield bonds. Risky or illiquid assets tend to have a distribution of returns that exhibits what is called *skewness* and excess *kurtosis*. We will first define these terms and then explain why it is necessary to understand their implications.

Skewness measures the asymmetry of a distribution. In other words, the historical pattern of returns does not resemble a normal (bell-curve) distribution. Negative skewness occurs when the values to the left of the mean (less than) are fewer but *farther* from the mean than are values to the right of the mean. For example: the return series of −30 percent, 5 percent, 10 percent, and 15 percent has a mean of 0 percent. There is only one return less than 0 percent, and three higher; but the one that is negative is much farther from zero than the positive ones. Positive skewness occurs when the values to the right of the mean (more than) are fewer but *farther* from the mean than are values to the left of the mean.

Behavioral finance studies have found that, in general, people like assets with positive skewness. This is evidenced by their willingness to accept low, or even negative, expected returns for assets that exhibit positive skewness. The classic example is a lottery ticket, which has negative expected returns. As we all know, there are precious few who win the lottery (positive outcome) and an enormous number who lose (negative outcome). However, the benefit of a positive outcome is much greater than the cost of a negative one. On the other hand, most people do not like assets with negative skewness. This explains why people generally purchase insurance against low-frequency events, such as disability or fires. While these events are unlikely to occur, they carry the potential for large losses. The problem for investors is that high-yield debt exhibits negative skewness.

High-yield debt returns also exhibit high kurtosis. Kurtosis measures the degree to which exceptional values, much larger or smaller than the average, occur more frequently (high kurtosis) or less frequently (low kurtosis) than in a normal (bell-shaped) distribution. High kurtosis results in exceptional values that are called "fat tails." Fat tails indicate a higher percentage of very low and very high returns than would be expected with a normal distribution. Low kurtosis results in "thin tails."

It is important for investors to understand that when skewness and kurtosis are present (the distribution of returns is not normal), investors looking *only* at the standard deviation of returns (the most commonly used measure of risk) receive a misleading picture of the riskiness of the asset class—understating the risks. This creates problems for investors and advisors using *efficient frontier models* (see glossary) to help them determine the "correct," or most efficient, asset allocation from a universe of risky assets. The reason is that efficient frontier models are based on *mean-variance analysis,* which assumes that investors care *only* about expected returns and the standard deviation. In other words, they do not care whether an asset exhibits skewness or kurtosis. If that assumption is correct (investors are not bothered by skewness and fat tails), then indeed, the use of mean-variance analysis is appropriate. However, this assumption is too simplistic, as many, if not most, investors do care about skewness (especially negative skewness) and kurtosis. If an asset exhibits nonnormal distribution (as do high-yield bonds), mean-variance analysis (using the standard deviation as the measure of risk) is only a good first approximation of risk, but does not completely reflect investors' true preferences. Mean-variance analysis will underestimate risk, and the result will be an overallocation to the asset class.

Asset Location

Investors holding high-yield securities in taxable accounts receive their incremental risk premium in the form of interest payments that are taxed at ordinary rates. If an investor holds that same distress risk in the form of equities, the return will be in the form of capital gains, which are taxed at lower long-term rates (or dividends which are now taxed at the same rate as long-term capital gains). On the other hand, because they have equity risks, holding high-yield securities in a tax-deferred account has negative implications.

It is preferable to hold equity risk in a taxable account for the following reasons.

- Holding equities (or equity risk) in tax-deferred accounts converts long-term gains into ordinary income upon withdrawal.
- Holding equities in taxable accounts creates the potential for a step-up in basis upon death to avoid estate taxes.
- Holding equities in taxable accounts allows for tax-loss harvesting to occur.
- Holding equities in taxable accounts allows for the gifting of securities to charities at the full value, thus avoiding taxes on gains.

These benefits are lost when you hold equity risks inside of a tax-deferred account, whether the equity risk is in the form of a bond or a stock.

A Risk Worth Taking?

In his wonderful book *Deep Survival,* Laurence Gonzales described the following situation. Eight snowmobilers had just completed a search-and-rescue mission. On their way back, they stopped at the base of a hill well known as great for climbing and hammerheading, a competitive game to see who can reach the highest point. The idea is to race up the hill until gravity stops you or you turn back downhill. This particular hill had a reputation for being especially dangerous and was prone to avalanches. Hammerheading was out of the question. Still, one of the snowmobilers could not resist temptation, and then a second could not resist the thrill of the hunt. An avalanche occurred and, tragically, two members of the team died.[3] This story reminds us that some risks are just not worth taking.

In summary, investing in high-yield bonds is a risk that is just not worth taking—the benefit of the higher yield is more than offset by the risks and other negatives that we have discussed. If investors seek greater returns than offered by investment-grade securities, they should do so by increasing either their equity allocation or their allocations to the riskier asset classes of small-cap stocks and value stocks. At the very least, if investors decide to hold high-yield debt, then they should be sure to adjust their allocations to include the recognition that they are taking some incremental equity risk. Finally, since diversification takes on greater significance as we move to lower-rated credits, investors who want to speculate with high-yield bonds should only consider doing so through a low-cost mutual fund like that offered by Vanguard. There is no other way to obtain sufficient diversification.

Preferred Stocks

Preferred stocks are technically equity investments, standing behind debt holders in the credit lineup. While preferred shareholders receive preference over common equity holders (hence the term "preferred"), in the case of a Chapter XI bankruptcy all debt holders would have to be paid off before any payment could be made to the preferred shareholders. If the company were to be liquidated, both preferred and common stockholders would generally receive nothing. Unlike with shares of common stock, which may benefit from the potential growth in the value of a company, the investment return on preferred stocks is a function of the fixed dividend yield (most preferred stocks carry a fixed yield). The difference is that conventional bonds have a fixed maturity date while preferred stocks may not.

Preferred stocks are either perpetual (have no maturity) or they are generally long-term, typically with a maturity of between thirty and fifty years. In addition, many issues with a stated maturity of thirty years include an issuer option to extend for an additional nineteen years. Investors considering purchasing a perpetual preferred should ask themselves the following question: Would a prudent investor purchase a bond from the same company paying the same interest rate with a hundred-year maturity? The answer is almost certainly no. Why not? Because the *credit risk* on a bond of such long maturity is likely to be too great. The very long term of preferred stocks with a stated maturity also creates a problem. As we discussed, the historical evidence on the risk and rewards of fixed-income investing is that longer maturities have the poorest risk-reward characteristics—the lowest return for a given level of risk.

Call Risk

The long maturity typical of preferred stocks is not the only problem with these securities; they typically also carry a call provision. With very few exceptions, U.S. Treasury debt has no call provision. Thus almost all U.S. government debt (as well as all noncallable debt instruments) has what is called *symmetric price risk.* If interest rates rise, bond prices will fall. If rates fall, bond prices will rise. A one percent rise or fall in interest rates will result in approximately a one percent change in the price of the bond for each year of duration. This is not the case with callable preferred stock. If rates rise, the price of the preferred will fall. However, if rates fall, and the issuer is able to do so, they will call the preferred and replace it with either a new preferred issue at lower rates, less expensive conventional debt, or perhaps even equity. Thus you have *asymmetric* risk: You get the risk of a long-duration product when rates rise, but because of the call feature when rates fall the gains are limited to the gains that would be realized from an instrument of shorter maturity. Thus preferred stocks rarely trade much above their issue price.

It is important to note that almost all callable preferred stocks are callable at par, thus there is an extremely limited upside potential (virtually none if the call date is near) if the security is purchased at par. Having protection from calls is vital to income-oriented investors because callable instruments present *reinvestment risk*, the risk of having to reinvest the proceeds of a called investment at lower rates. Through calls investors lose access to relatively higher income streams. Thus part of the incremental yield of preferred stocks relative to a noncallable debt issuance of the same company is compensation for giving the issuer the right to call the debt should the rate environment prove favorable. The other source of the incremental yield of preferred stocks is the credit risk.

Credit Risk

To begin, as is the case with corporate bonds, preferred stocks are rated by the four major credit-rating agencies. This makes it easy to check the credit quality, although, as is also the case with corporate bonds, the rating needs to be constantly monitored. While all preferred stocks are not in the junk bond category, they seldom are highly rated credits (though there are exceptions). Given the lower cost of tax-deductible conventional debt (as equity preferred dividends are not deductible for the issuer) one has to ask why companies issue preferred stock, especially when traditionally preferred shares are rated two notches below the issuer's rating on unsecured debt (the lower credit rating increases the cost). The answer is often not very reassuring to investors; they may issue preferred stocks because they have already loaded their balance sheet with a large amount of debt and risk a downgrade if they pile on even more.

Some companies issue preferred stock for regulatory reasons. For example, regulators might limit the amount of debt a company is allowed to have outstanding. There might also exist other regulatory reasons. In October 1996 the Federal Reserve allowed U.S. bank holding companies to treat certain types of preferred stocks (what are called hybrid preferred stocks) as Tier 1 capital for capital adequacy purposes. An additional reason for issuing preferred stock is that it can be structured to look like debt from a tax perspective and equity from a balance sheet perspective. Instruments structured in this manner are called trust preferreds. Finally, investors should be aware that preferred dividends are paid at the discretion of the company. Thus in times of financial distress preferred dividends could be deferred. On the other hand, bond interest payments represent a contractual obligation, and failure to pay sets the wheels in motion for reorganization or bankruptcy and liquidation.

There is another risk associated with buying preferred stocks that is related to the call feature. The call feature is not only related, as most investors think, to interest rate risk, but also to changes in the company's credit rating. An issuer with a low-rated credit and a high-yielding preferred will likely call the preferred if their credit status improves—and replace the preferred with a now higher-rated conventional corporate bond (and its tax deductibility). Of course, if the company's credit deteriorates, it will not call the preferred (but the price of the preferred will fall due to the deteriorated credit). Again, an asymmetric risk for the investor—one of the reasons for the higher yield. Risk and *ex-ante* reward are always related. Whether the higher yield eventually translates into higher returns, and for how long, is a question to which only a clear crystal ball could provide the answer.

Investors can benefit from learning to think of things from the company's perspective. Most companies with solid credit ratings generally will not issue preferred stocks (except for regulatory reasons) since the dividend payments are not tax-deductible like bond interest. Thus preferred stocks are generally too expensive a form of capital for strong credits. Thus before buying a preferred an investor might ask why a company would issue preferred stock paying a generous dividend when they could presumably issue debt securities with more favorable tax consequences. Investors seeking safe returns are generally not going to like the answer.

There is another point we need to cover. Longer-term maturities with fixed yields do provide a hedge against deflationary environments. The problem with long-maturity preferred stocks is that the call feature negates the benefits of the longer maturity in a falling rate environment. Thus the holder does not benefit from a rise in price that would occur with a noncallable fixed-rate security in a falling rate environment. If the issuer is unable to call the preferred, the reason is likely to be a deteriorating credit rating, putting the investor's principal at risk. Given that preferred issuers are generally companies with weaker credit ratings, and distressed companies are the very ones most likely to default in deflationary environments, the benefit of the high-yielding longer maturity (which should rise in price in a falling rate environment) is unlikely to be realized by the holders of these callable instruments.

Are there any good reasons to buy a preferred stock? Corporate buyers of preferred stock receive favorable tax treatment on the dividends of preferred stock, with most of the dividend not subject to taxes. U.S. corporate holders can exclude up to 70 percent of the dividend from their taxable income provided they hold the shares at least forty-five days. This favorable tax treatment creates demand for the product. Individuals get no such favorable tax treatment.

The bottom line is that investors buying preferred stocks because of the higher yield, possibly combined with the fear of equity investing, are taking on additional risk. Since the market is very efficient at pricing risk, significantly higher yields must entail significantly greater risk (something fixed-income investors were likely seeking to avoid in the first place). These risks include perpetual life (or very long maturity), a call feature, low credit standing, deferrable dividends, and a depressed yield due to demand from corporations that receive favorable tax treatment.

Other Considerations

There are some other reasons to consider avoiding preferred stocks. First, there are no low-cost index or passive asset-class funds that provide investors with the most effective way to diversify the risks of individual issuers. Second, if you buy individual issues you have the trading costs involved, the lack of diversification, and the need to constantly monitor credit ratings. Third, the typical lengthy maturity of preferred issues increases credit risk. Many companies might present modest credit risk in the near term, but their credit risk increases over time. Finally, while fixed-rate noncallable debt makes an excellent diversifier for stock portfolios because a weak economy (which usually has a negative impact on stock prices) generally leads to falling interest rates and rising bond prices, due to their call feature preferred shares will not benefit as much.

Summary

The risks incurred when investing in preferred stocks make them inappropriate investments for individual investors. As we have discussed, fixed-income investors should stick with U.S. government debt and debt in the two highest credit-rating brackets, AAA and AA. If investors have the ability, willingness, or need to take more risk, that risk is best taken in the equity market, where it can be earned in a low-cost and highly tax-efficient manner.

Convertible Bonds

The same issues that apply to preferred securities also apply to convertible debt. Like preferreds (and high-yield bonds), convertible bonds are also often touted because of their nonperfect correlation with equities. However, as we have seen with high-yield bonds, low correlation is only a *necessary* condition for investors to consider a security. The *sufficient* condition is that the security provides the appropriate risk-adjusted expected returns given its role in the portfolio.

With convertible bonds you have the issue of equity risk being present and you also have a shifting asset allocation depending on where the stock price is trading relative to the conversion rate stated in the bond. If the current stock price is well above the conversion price, then you are basically holding an equity security—the convertible bond will move virtually in tandem with the stock price. On the other hand, if the price is well below the conversion price, then you are basically holding a debt instrument—the convertible will trade more like a bond than a stock.

The remaining maturity and the credit rating are also important factors in determining just how much equity and fixed-income risk you really are holding when owning a convertible bond. As these factors shift, your asset allocation will be shifting, causing you to lose control over the most significant determinant of the risk and expected reward of your portfolio. In addition, all of the negative tax implications (for individual investors) we discussed in connection with high-yield bonds and preferred stocks apply to convertible securities as well. Thus, once again, prudent investors should avoid including convertible securities (or any hybrid security) in a portfolio. As we have said, if investors want to seek, or need to seek, higher returns, then they should take the risk in the equity portion of their portfolios.

Having completed our review of corporate fixed-income securities, we next turn our attention to international bonds. We will first discuss them as a broad asset class and then move on to discuss the specific asset class of emerging-market bonds. When considering these asset classes we need to keep in mind the general principles of prudent fixed-income investing regarding term risk, credit risk, and the need for, and benefits of, diversification that we have already discussed.

CHAPTER EIGHT

◆

The World of International Fixed-Income Securities

The safest port in a sea of uncertainty is diversification.
— Ron Ross, *The Unbeatable Market*

I'm a big believer in diversification, because I am totally convinced that forecasts will be wrong. Diversification is the guiding principle. That's the only way you can live through the hard times. — Paul Samuelson

You've got to look at the portfolio as a whole, not just position by position. And if you're trying to reduce the volatility or uncertainty of your portfolio as a whole, then you need more than one security obviously, but you also need securities which don't go up and down together.
— Harry Markowitz, Nobel Prize winner in economics

Broad diversification of risk is one of the rules of prudent investing. For equity investors an important step in reducing the overall risk of equities is to include a very significant allocation to international equities in the portfolio. Both the historical evidence and the logic of diversification suggest that investors should allocate as much as 30 to 50 percent of their equity holdings to international equities, including a small allocation to emerging-market equities. It seems logical, therefore, that investors should also consider allocating a significant portion of their fixed-income portfolios to international securities. This is the issue we will now consider.

We begin by understanding that there are two main types of fixed-income risks that we might want to diversify, credit and interest rate risk. U.S. investors can eliminate the need for diversification of *credit risk* by limiting their holdings to those that carry the full faith and credit of the U.S. government. Thus, in terms of credit risk, international diversification does not provide any diversification benefit to investors who choose that route.

That leaves us with the following question: Is there a potential diversification benefit in terms of *interest rate risk*? The answer, as you will see, is that it depends. It depends on whether the international bond is a U.S. dollar bond or is denominated in a foreign currency. If the instrument is a U.S. dollar bond, then its price movement (other than a movement caused by a change in credit risk) will reflect the movement in U.S. interest rates. Thus no diversification benefit in terms of interest rate risk is provided. On the other hand, if the issue is denominated in a foreign currency, then any price movement (in foreign currency terms) caused by interest rate changes will come from changes in the level of interest rates in the country of which the currency is denominated, and not from changes in U.S. rates. The bond markets of various countries do not typically move in the same direction, or by similar amounts, at the same time. Sometimes U.S. bond markets are rallying (interest rates falling) while foreign bond markets are falling. And sometimes the reverse is true. Thus owning bonds denominated in foreign currencies can provide a diversification benefit—thereby reducing volatility, without reducing expected return. This benefit, however, comes at the price of accepting currency risk—the risk that a foreign currency will fall in value relative to the dollar (of course, it can also rise in value).

Currency Risk

The issue of currency risk is a complex one. We begin by understanding that foreign currency risk is not necessarily a good or a bad thing. In addition, currency risk is a different type of risk than equity risk, credit risk, or duration risk. Unlike these risks, currency risk has no expected return, and therefore has no risk premium. However, currency risk may increase the volatility of the portfolio—though the historical evidence suggests that this has not been the case, at least when it comes to equity investing.[1] It is the issue of volatility that should concern the fixed-income investor.

Consider that the main purpose of fixed-income assets is to either create a safety net of highly stable assets that allow us to take equity risk while sleeping well, or to create a highly stable stream of income needed to provide a desired lifestyle with a minimum amount of risk. Because currency values relative to the U.S. dollar can be volatile, owning foreign currency denominated bonds will at times increase the volatility of both the value of the asset and the income stream we desire to provide us with stability. Thus it would seem that owning a foreign currency denominated bond would be at odds with our objective of stability. Fortunately, there is a simple solution—currency risk can be hedged (protected against) in the foreign currency markets. These markets are about the most liquid in the world, and as long as one limits holdings to the currencies of the major developed markets (e.g., Canada, France, Germany, Japan, the U.K.) the cost of hedging will be minimal. That is, it will be minimal if you are an institutional investor with access to the wholesale markets. Buying foreign currency denominated debt instruments and hedging the currency risk allows investors to receive the benefit of diversification of interest rate risk because the volatility of the overall fixed-income portfolio is reduced. Since we can reduce volatility without reducing expected returns, we have achieved our objective.

Diversifying Interest Rate Risk

Individuals considering owning international fixed-income assets should understand that in order to effectively diversify interest rate risk (and credit risk) an investor would need to own bonds denominated in several currencies. The most cost-effective way to accomplish this objective is to own a low-cost mutual fund. In addition to the diversification benefit a mutual fund provides, another reason to utilize a fund is that the cost of hedging the currency risk would almost certainly be much greater for individuals than it is for institutional investors. The difference is a result of the markup a retail investor would pay over the wholesale (or interdealer) price. As is the case with the market for municipal bonds, in the foreign exchange markets, size matters. That is, small trades pay large markups. And the interdealer foreign exchange market trades in blocks of at least $1 million.

To summarize, owning currency-hedged foreign denominated bonds is an effective way to gain exposure to foreign interest rate cycles that are different from U.S. interest rate cycles without taking the currency risk. Investors seeking the diversification benefit, and possibly somewhat higher returns of investing in high-grade foreign bonds, should do so only through mutual funds that can effectively diversify the risk of owning a single issuer, and also hedge the foreign currency risk in a low-cost manner. It should also be a passively managed fund, since there is no evidence of ability of active managers to add value in this asset class. The fund would also have to fit the desired maturity structure of the investor (and again it is recommended that maturities be limited to the short and intermediate term). In addition, the fund should limit its holdings to the two highest investment grades (AAA and AA). The major rating agencies do provide ratings on foreign bonds as well as on U.S. bonds. Morningstar, for example, has a service that allows you to check the credit quality of the holdings of a bond mutual fund.

A Word of Caution

The credit ratings of the bonds of foreign governments can change very rapidly. Just two years before the Asian crisis that hit the markets in 1998 the credit rating of Malaysia was AA+, and the rating of Thailand was AAA.[2] (Both were sharply downgraded by the rating agencies.) This warning is not meant to frighten investors away from considering owning international fixed-income assets. However, it does serve two critical reminders. The first is that prudent investors must always keep in mind that even the highly unlikely (a AAA-rated bond going into default) is not impossible. Thus diversification of risk is an essential part of a prudent strategy. And second, with the assets that are meant to provide stability of value or stability of cash flow we should seek to minimize credit risk. With that in mind, our recommendation is to limit fixed-income investments to the major industrial countries, and to limit even their maturities to the short to intermediate term.

Emerging-Market Bonds

Every age has its peculiar folly: some scheme, project, or fantasy into which it plunges, spurred on by the love of gain, the necessity of excitement, or the force of imitation.
—Charles MacKay, *Extraordinary Popular Delusions and the Madness of Crowds,* 1841

During the 2000–02 bear market for equities one of the top-performing asset classes was emerging-market bonds. While the global equities markets (including emerging-market equities) were suffering, many emerging-market bond funds provided double-digit returns. The question for prudent investors is the following: Are emerging-market bonds an appropriate building block for a globally diversified portfolio? Let's examine the issues that lead to the conclusion that they are not appropriate vehicles for individual investors.

Risks

Emerging-market debt is a very risky asset class, characterized by very high volatility. In fact, for the period January 1991–September 1999, emerging-market debt exhibited greater volatility than emerging-market equities (though returns were higher as well).[3] Note that because emerging-market debt is similar in nature to the asset class of high-yield bonds, it should not be surprising that the issues investors should consider are basically the same. We are, therefore, confronted with the same three characteristics that risk-averse investors should find unattractive.

First, emerging-market bond returns exhibit negative *skewness*. Second, emerging-market bond returns exhibit high *kurtosis*. Risk-averse investors prefer a distribution with low kurtosis (i.e., returns do not vary far from the mean). Having both negative skewness and high kurtosis is a sign of a highly risky asset class—there is the potential for very large losses. Recalling our discussion of high-yield bonds, remember that if an asset exhibits nonnormal distribution (as do high-yield bonds), mean-variance analysis (looking at standard deviation as the measure of risk) is only a good first approximation of risk, but does not completely reflect investors' true preferences.

Third, the securities markets for emerging-market debt are not very liquid. This means that not only are trading costs very high, but also in times of crises markets can virtually dry up. Buyers totally disappear and sales cannot be made at any price. And in the case of emerging markets, crises are not an infrequent occurrence. In addition, we need to remember that portfolios of illiquid securities have reported returns that tend to be smoother than true economic returns, resulting in the understatement of volatility and the overstatement of risk-adjusted performance measures such as the Sharpe ratio.

Finally, investors can also make the mistake of being fooled by a period of high returns into thinking the asset class is not risky. One day the risk shows up and all the "excess" returns earned can disappear.

Correlation of Returns to Other Asset Classes

An asset class that is risky in isolation may be less so in the context of the overall portfolio if it exhibits low correlation with other asset classes. On the positive side, there are periods when emerging-market bonds exhibit low correlation with other asset classes, even emerging-market equities. These are periods characterized by tranquillity in the economies (and politics) of the emerging-market countries. Unfortunately, the correlation of returns tends to increase during times of crises, which is just the wrong time for investors. The perfect example occurred during the summer of 1998 when the world experienced a global capital markets crisis. In just the month of August of that year JP Morgan's Emerging Market Bond Index fell almost 26 percent.[4] It is during periods of crises that emerging-market bonds have high correlation with emerging-market equities. Just when we need low correlation, we may get high correlation. Thus we see a similar story to what happens with U.S. high-yield debt; in times of crises debt issues with low credit ratings become highly correlated with the equity of the issuer. In emerging markets, the lower the credit rating of the country, the greater the correlation of returns with the equity markets of that country.[5]

Attraction

The main attraction for investors is the high coupon that emerging-market bonds carry. However, investors need to remember the following:

- The high coupon is a reflection of the very high risk that these securities entail.
- The high coupon does not equal the expected return. The risk of default and expected losses must be considered.
- The high coupon is not only compensation for the significant credit risk entailed, but also for the lack of liquidity and the high trading costs that are incurred when buying and selling.
- The risks of emerging-market bonds tend to show up just when equity assets in the portfolio are experiencing distress.

Other Considerations

- Since the return of emerging-market debt is in the form of current income, the asset class is a tax-inefficient one. Thus it should be held in a tax-deferred account. Holding this asset class in a tax-deferred account has some negative implications. First, because of the high volatility of the asset class, there are likely to be opportunities to tax-loss harvest. This can only be done in a taxable account. Second, all income from tax-deferred accounts is ultimately taxed as ordinary income. Instead of holding emerging-market bonds, an investor could take similar risk and hold emerging-market equity in a taxable account, the returns from which would be taxed at lower long-term capital gains rates.

- There are no passive, low-cost investment vehicles to implement an emerging-market bond strategy. The only choices available are actively managed funds. Actively managed funds tend not only to be high cost, but also typically to have highly concentrated (risky) holdings. The table below provides the operating expense ratio, the turnover rate, and the top ten holdings as a percent of total assets for five popular funds. It is especially important to note the turnover rates because the low levels of liquidity in this asset class can lead

Emerging-Market Bond Funds

Emerging-Market Bond Fund	Operating Expense Ratio	Turnover	Top Ten Holdings as Percent of Total Assets
Alliance	1.47%	125%	53
Payden	0.86%	187%	45
PIMCO	1.25%	461%	31
T. R. Price	1.10%	69%	46
Van Kampen World	1.55%	228%	25

Source: Morningstar as of December 2004

to high trading costs (both bid-offer spreads and market-impact costs).

- There is another consideration regarding the use of actively managed funds in this asset class. Actively managed funds, at least in theory, can exploit market mispricings. A problem for actively managed funds in this asset class is that it is virtually the exclusive domain of sophisticated institutional investors, including mutual funds, hedge funds, pension plans, and investment banks. Thus there does not seem to be a likely group of victims whose lack of knowledge can be exploited to help offset the high costs mentioned above.

- It is highly unlikely that the high returns experienced from 2000 to 2002 can be repeated. First, during the crisis of 1998 the spread between the yields on emerging-market debt and U.S. Treasury debt dramatically widened. Since the crisis was resolved in a favorable manner, spreads have narrowed. While this narrowing can continue, at some point it must come to an end because of the risky nature of the asset class. Thus spread narrowings should be treated as one-time gains, not as permanent risk premiums. Second, the yield on U.S. Treasury securities fell dramatically between 2000 and 2003. Since emerging-market debt trades at a spread over U.S. Treasury debt, and therefore their yields fell in tandem with U.S. Treasury yields, this, too, must be treated as a onetime event, not likely to be an ongoing occurrence.

- The main purpose for fixed-income assets within the context of the overall portfolio is typically to allow investors to take the amount of equity risk with which they are comfortable.

Emerging-market bonds are certainly not an asset class that can be relied on to help investors sleep well during periods when equity markets are experiencing distress.

Summary

The performance record of emerging-market bonds during the bear market of 2000–02 attracted many return-chasing investors to the asset class. There are positive attributes that make this asset class worth considering as a building block in a globally diversified portfolio—the high expected return combined with low correlation to both high credit quality U.S. debt securities and to U.S. and international equities. On the other hand, there are many negatives for investors (especially risk-averse investors) to consider: the high volatility; the likelihood of negative fat tails; the tendency of correlations to rise at the wrong time; and the very high costs of implementing an emerging-market bond strategy. The bottom line is that for fixed-income investors the negatives appear to substantially outweigh the positives. While including emerging-market bonds in a portfolio is not recommended, for those wishing to do so the following suggestions are offered:

- Because of the high-risk nature of the asset class, any allocation to emerging-market bonds should be considered an allocation to equities and not fixed income.
- Choose the active fund with the combination of the lowest expense ratio and, because trading costs are very high in this asset class, the lowest historical turnover (keeping in mind that the past turnover of actively managed funds may not be a good predictor of future turnover).
- Avoid load funds because loads act as a drag on returns.

We have now completed our review of the world of international fixed-income investments. The next chapter focuses on one of the largest and fastest growing fixed-income markets, the world of mortgage-backed securities.

CHAPTER NINE

◆

The World of Mortgage-Backed Securities

Don't invest in new or "interesting" investments. They are designed to be sold to investors, not to be owned by investors.
— Charles Ellis, *Investment Policy*

One of the more popular forms of fixed-income investing is residential mortgage-backed securities, with trillions of dollars now invested in them. Their popularity is based on both the high credit quality of most of these securities and the incremental yield they provide over similarly rated bonds with the same *expected* maturity. As you should know by now, the incremental yield is compensation for taking incremental risks related to the *expected* maturity of the security.

A rule that prudent investors should always follow is to never invest in a security the risks of which they do not fully understand. Unfortunately, most investors do not fully understand the nature of the risks of investing in mortgage-backed securities. This chapter explains the nature of these instruments and the risks involved. With this knowledge we can then determine if these securities are appropriate for inclusion in a prudent fixed-income portfolio.

Mortgage-backed securities (MBS) are sometimes called "mortgage pass-through certificates." This is because the security *passes through* to investors, at a specific coupon, the principal and interest scheduled for payment each month from mortgagors on the outstanding balance of the loans backing the security. It also *passes through* any unscheduled prepayments.

An investor in an MBS owns an undivided interest in a pool of mortgages that serves as the underlying asset for the security. As an MBS holder, the investor receives a pro-rata share of the cash flows from the pool of mortgages. A nationwide network of lenders such as mortgage bankers, savings and loan associations, and commercial banks originate the loans backing the MBS. These lenders submit groups of similar mortgage loans to an issuer for securitization. The loans are converted—or securitized—into tradable and highly liquid instruments. Once the loans have been securitized, dealers sell the MBS to investors, both institutional and individual. Ginnie Mae, Fannie Mae, and Freddie Mac issue most MBS. MBS issued by these three entities carry a guarantee of timely payment of principal and interest to the investor, whether or not there is sufficient cash flow from the underlying group of mortgages.

From a credit safety perspective, the safest of these issuers is Ginnie Mae. Their obligations are backed by the full faith and credit of the United States. Fannie Mae and Freddie Mac are unique institutions. As we have discussed, while they are public companies, they are considered *quasi*-government agencies. Their obligations do not carry the full faith and credit of the U.S. government. However, their bonds are very highly rated (AAA). In addition, because of the nature of the collateral, the *MBS* they issue are considered of even greater credit quality than AAA-rated GSE *bonds*.

The growth of the MBS market has been explosive, with over $3 trillion now outstanding. Money managers, thrift institutions, commercial banks, trust departments, insurance companies, pension funds, securities dealers, other major corporations, and private investors are all players in this market.

What makes MBS so attractive to investors? The attraction is the higher stated yields they carry compared to other forms of fixed-income investing of comparable credit quality. The higher yields, and thus the greater *expected* returns, come at the price, however, of greater risk. That risk is not in the form of credit risk, but, instead, takes the form of interest rate and duration (maturity) risk. The reason is that the maturity of an MBS is uncertain. Let's explore the issue of the duration risk incurred when purchasing an MBS. Understanding the nature of the risks will help you determine if they are appropriate investments for your portfolio.

Risks

Despite their popularity, the risks of investing in MBS are not fully (if at all) understood by most investors. The reason is that MBS, especially MBS derivatives such as collateralized mortgage obligations (CMOs), can be highly complex instruments. All that most investors see are the higher coupons. The high coupon rate, the historically higher returns these investments have provided, and the historically excellent performance of MBS with strong credit ratings (Ginnie Maes carry a *U.S. government guarantee* of timely payment of principal and interest) attract investors to these securities. While they have some positive attributes, there are significant risks in MBS.

As we have said, almost all U.S. Treasury debt has a fixed and certain maturity. There are very few remaining U.S. Treasury debt obligations that contain a call provision. The Treasury has not issued callable securities since 1985. Thus U.S. Treasury debt (as well as all noncallable debt instruments) has what is called *positive convexity*—duration increases (shortens) when rates fall (rise). If interest rates rise (fall), bond prices will fall (rise). For each year of duration, a one percent rise or fall in interest rates will result in approximately the same change in the price of the bond. However, because the expected maturity of an MBS depends to a great degree on the current level of interest rates relative to the level at the time the mortgages backing the MBS were originated, an MBS can exhibit *negative convexity*—duration actually shortens when rates fall. In order to bring clarity to this issue we will examine how changes in interest rates impact the value of an MBS.

Let's assume you purchase a newly issued Ginnie Mae with a coupon of 7 percent. Let's also assume that based on that interest rate the Ginnie Mae has an *average expected* life of seven years. The term *average* is important because it is assumed that some of the underlying mortgages will prepay sooner and some will last longer. The term *expected* is important because we cannot know in advance what the *actual* average life will turn out to be. The actual average life will depend not only on any changes in interest rates, but also on levels of economic activity. Let's also assume that a Treasury bond with seven years left to maturity is yielding 6.5 percent, one-half percent below that of your Ginnie Mae. Thus you are receiving a risk premium (higher *expected* return) of one-half percent. Of course, when the MBS eventually matures we don't know if you will have earned that premium for the full expected life or not. Your return over the seven years may even turn out to be less than that of the seven-year Treasury note. Let's see why this is so.

If interest rates fall 1 percent so that a newly issued Ginnie Mae is yielding just 6 percent, the average expected life of your Ginnie Mae will shorten as principal repayments occur at a faster than expected rate. This happens as investors take advantage of lower rates either to move and take advantage of a now lower-rate mortgage, or to refinance their existing loan. Thus while the 7 percent MBS will initially rise in price, it will not rise in price as fast as a Treasury bond that has the same maturity. And when the MBS pays off, you will then have to reinvest the proceeds for the remaining term at a now lower rate, possibly a lot lower than the 6½ percent you could have been earning on a Treasury note that had no prepayment risk. But this is not the end of our story. The reason is that if rates rise, the risks can be even greater.

Let us now assume that rates rise so that the current coupon Ginnie Mae is yielding 9 percent. While the price of the Treasury bond you could have purchased will fall, the price of the Ginnie Mae will fall even farther. The reason is that the bond's maturity will have remained the same but now the expected maturity of the Ginnie Mae has lengthened. With higher rates mortgagors will tend to stay in their current homes longer to avoid paying higher rates if they moved, and current homeowners will not refinance— and the longer the maturity, the greater the price move for any given change in interest rate levels.

As you can see MBS have *asymmetric* risk. The investor in an MBS has in effect sold a continuous call to the borrower because the borrower has the right to prepay at any time. The result is that the life of the MBS can be shorter than expected at issuance. If rates rise, however, the expected life of the MBS will lengthen due to the borrower's ability to extend the *expected* stay in her current home, leaving the lender earning below market rates. The price the owner of the MBS received for accepting both of these risks is the incremental yield over a Treasury bond that has the same maturity as the *expected* average maturity of the MBS upon its issuance. That incremental yield is a risk premium. In fact, the only way you collect that risk premium is if rates stay in a relatively narrow band. Otherwise you get the worst of all worlds. When rates rise, you are holding an investment whose duration is lengthening at just the wrong time. When rates fall, you are holding an investment whose duration is shortening at just the wrong time. And this risk is even greater than it seems when you look at an MBS in isolation. The reason is that the risks of an MBS can show up at exactly the wrong time in relation to what is happening with your equity holdings. For example, rising interest rates, caused by rising inflation, would likely have a negative impact on both stocks and MBS.

As you can see from the above examples MBS are very complex securities. In fact, when we consider purchasing an MBS we cannot even know the yield-to-maturity—we can only guess at it. When the yield on an MBS (e.g., a Ginnie Mae) is quoted, the calculation is based on a rate of prepayment *assumption*. The rate of prepayment used to make the yield calculation is an estimate by the market based on historic evidence. The industry standard generally used for yield calculations is called the PSA (Public Securities Association) model. How the model works is beyond the scope of this book. However, it is vital that investors understand that a quoted yield is only as good as the assumptions turn out to be (and those assumptions are changing all the time).

Correlation with Equities

As was discussed earlier, the longer the duration of a fixed-income instrument, the higher the correlation of its returns with the return of equities. Thus in a rising rate environment, because duration is increasing, MBS will have increasing correlation with equities, and this is not a good thing. Rising rates can negatively impact stock prices. Thus just when you need fixed-income assets to protect you, your MBS is falling in value and becoming more risky as its maturity lengthens. On the other hand, in a falling rate environment longer maturities would be helpful. However, your MBS is shortening in maturity at the wrong time, and reinvestment risk will show up.

It is important to note that the call (prepayment) risk results in an MBS rarely trading much above its issue price. Having protection from calls (which almost all Treasury debt and most corporate debt have) is critical to income-oriented investors because callable instruments present *reinvestment risk,* the risk of having to reinvest the proceeds of a called investment at a lower rate. Through calls investors lose access to relatively higher income streams. Thus part of the incremental yield of an MBS relative to noncallable debt is compensation for giving the borrower the right to prepay should the rate environment prove favorable. There is one more point we need to cover regarding the risks of MBS.

When interest rates begin to fall, newly issued MBS will initially rise in price, as they will carry a greater than market interest rate. Mutual funds that own MBS will often buy these bonds at a price that will be above par (above 100). The reason is that they can then advertise a higher yield for their fund. Unsophisticated investors are then attracted to the higher yield. However, in most cases, they do not understand the risks. If rates continue to fall, the price of the above-par bond might actually begin to fall as the prepayment risk increases. This is exactly what happened in the crash of October 1987. Investors in high-coupon MBS that paid above par actually lost principal when interest rates collapsed because the price of their bonds fell. This is an example of the asymmetric risk of MBS. Not only did investors lose large sums, but they also experienced these losses at the same time their equities had collapsed in value. Another reason why we want our fixed-income assets to have low correlation, not high correlation, with equities.

The Role of MBS in a Portfolio

Now that the risks of MBS have been explained we can determine if they make appropriate investments for a portfolio. From a credit risk perspective MBS, as long as the issuers are Ginnie Mae, Fannie Mae, or Freddie Mac, are prudent investments that meet our criteria. However, from the perspective of price risk, reinvestment risk, and correlation with equities they cannot be recommended. In addition, unless you fully understand all of the risks discussed above, you should not consider investing in MBS.

If you do wish to try to earn the risk premium that MBS carry, the vehicle of choice is the Vanguard Ginnie Mae Fund. Individual MBS should almost certainly be avoided for a variety of reasons. First, MBS are complex issues and it is unlikely an investor will understand all of the risks. Second, pricing in the market is opaque, and investors are likely to pay large markups. Third, if an investor had to sell prior to maturity they would likely experience very high trading costs. A mutual fund will receive much better pricing when buying and selling than will an individual investor. And with a mutual fund, investors always trade at the NAV.

We need to cover one last point. Vanguard's Total Bond Market Fund includes about a one-third allocation to MBS. Therefore, we cannot recommend the fund. The first reason is that the duration of the Treasury and corporate bonds in the fund is greater than preferred. Second, the fund does contain MBS and has the associated risks.

Before concluding our discussion of MBS, there is a specialized category of MBS that we need to discuss.

Collateralized Mortgage Obligations

Within the broad asset class of mortgage-backed securities there is a more specific type called collateralized mortgage obligations, or CMOs. A CMO is a mortgage-backed bond that separates pools of fixed-rate mortgages into different expected maturity classes. The collateral for a CMO can be either residential or commercial mortgages. The structure of CMOs redistributes the risks associated with prepayments and extensions because each security is divided into classes that are paid off in order. These risks are reduced for the early maturity classes and increased for the latter ones. Each class is called a *tranche*. Tranches can be differentiated by the expected maturity as well as by the type of return. A given tranche may receive only interest, only principal, or a combination of the two. CMOs may even include more complex stipulations.

The first tranche of a CMO must be paid off before the second tranche receives any principal payments. Thus the first tranche has the greatest protection against the risk of the expected maturity extending. The protection against extension risk decreases as the tranches progress. The increased extension protection for the early tranches leads, of course, to greater extension risk for the lower-level tranches, the ones with the longer expected maturity. As we would expect, in return for the reduction in prepayment risk (increased predictability of payments) CMOs with greater predictability of maturity provide lower yields than do other MBS.

One negative of CMOs is that they are generally illiquid instruments. The illiquidity increases the cost of buying and selling them, making them inappropriate investments for all but the investor who is virtually certain he or she will be able to buy and hold until maturity. Another negative is the lack of transparency of pricing, which can lead to investors being exploited through large markups and markdowns.

Another strong warning is warranted about CMOs. CMOs are generally structured to meet the specific cash flow objectives of institutional investors. They are the ones who are sold the tranches that have the best risk characteristics. What is left is known in the industry as the "toxic waste." Those are the tranches that get sold to the public. Unless you (or your fee-only advisor) have the depth of knowledge to separate the wheat from the chaff, CMOs should be avoided.

The bottom line with CMOs is that the tranche structure that provides the reduction in uncertainty of maturity makes these instruments (at least the early tranches) look more like conventional fixed-income investments with known maturities. The more the structure increases the certainty of the timing of payments, the more straight-debt-like the investment becomes. The result is that the yield premium in a tightly structured CMO becomes mostly a payment for the liquidity the investor gives up and for the increased trading costs that may be incurred. This might make them attractive for institutional buy-and-hold investors who can purchase them at wholesale prices—something it is not likely an individual investor will be able to accomplish.

Like all taxable fixed-income investments CMOs should be held in a tax-deferred or nontaxable account. A tax-deferred account is a logical place to hold an illiquid investment because the funds in these accounts generally serve long-term purposes and are unlikely to be tapped except in an emergency (unless the investor is in the distribution stage). The illiquid nature of these instruments also precludes them as appropriate investments for individuals to buy directly, as the trading costs (markups and bid-offer spreads) are too great. However, for investors who have access to the wholesale (or interdealer) market through their investment manager or investment advisor, CMOs offer an opportunity to increase yields. If an investor is willing to accept that they will have to buy and hold the instrument, early tranche CMOs (with short expected maturity) may be appropriate for a small percentage of their fixed-income allocation. Only the shorter-term tranches should be considered because the longer-term ones have similar risk of maturity problems (though exacerbated) to all MBS, and the longer maturities increase the correlation with the equity portion of the portfolio. Once again, it is recommended that investors consider only CMOs that are backed by the MBS of GNMA, Fannie Mae, or Freddie Mac, or ones that carry a AAA or AA rating.

We have now completed our survey of the asset class of taxable fixed-income securities and are ready to move on to the world of municipal bonds.

CHAPTER TEN

◆

The World of Municipal Bonds

*For all long-term investors, there is only one objective—
maximum total real return after taxes.*
    —John Templeton, founder of the Templeton Group

As you have learned, much of the conventional wisdom about investing in general, and fixed-income investing specifically, is wrong. Unfortunately, the conventional wisdom that municipal bonds are appropriate investments for only those investors in the highest tax bracket falls into that category of bad advice. In fact, there are times when even investors in the lowest tax brackets should consider owning municipal bonds. This chapter will provide you with the knowledge needed to determine whether municipal bonds are the appropriate choice and to decide on a prudent investment strategy.

We have already covered a substantial amount of information related to investing in municipal bonds. We begin, therefore, with a review of that material. We will then move on to discuss other issues that need to be understood in order to develop an appropriate strategy. The following is a summary of the issues that we have covered to this point.

Taxes

- Interest income from municipal bonds is generally exempt from federal income taxes. However, some municipal bonds, because they are considered private activity bonds, are subject to the federal alternative minimum tax (AMT).

- Interest income from municipal bonds is generally exempt from state and local taxes if the bond issuer is from the same state as the residency of the investor. Some states provide that exemption to the bonds of other states. On the other hand, a small number of states tax interest even on their own bonds (e.g., Wisconsin and Illinois).

- The tax-exempt status of municipal bonds creates the need to compare the taxable equivalent yield on municipal bonds to the yield on taxable instruments of similar maturity and credit quality.

- Bonds bought at a discount are subject to ordinary income taxes on the amount of the discount unless it falls within the de minimis rule. Thus part of the return may be subject to federal income taxes.

Price Risk

- Discount bonds (the kind most individual investors prefer to buy) are subject to greater price risk than are premium bonds of the same maturity.

- Most intermediate to long-term municipal bonds have call features. Thus investors must consider the call risk when evaluating the appropriateness of a bond. The yield-to-worst should be considered as well as the yield-to-maturity.

- Many municipal bonds have a sinking fund provision, creating the risk of early redemption.

Yield Curve

There are several factors contributing to the fact that the yield curve for municipal bonds is generally much steeper than it is for Treasury bonds. The first is the tax, or regulatory, risk discussed in chapter 2. The second is that municipal bonds entail credit risk, while Treasury bonds do not—and the longer the maturity, the greater the credit risk. The third reason is that there is a supply-demand imbalance in the municipal bond market. The supply of long-term debt is much greater from issuers (who seek to match the maturity of the debt with the long-term nature of their assets) than there is demand from buyers. The result is that the "sweet spot" of the municipal bond yield curve is generally farther out for municipals than it is for Treasuries.

Credit Risk

- Municipal bonds have significantly less credit risk than do similarly rated corporate bonds.
- Municipal bonds of the highest credit rating (AAA or AA) that have the same rating and the same maturity are highly likely (though not certain) to provide the same *pretax* return because they experience almost no defaults. (A difference between the supply-demand relationship for the bonds of the various states can lead to differences in yields of bonds of the same maturity and the same credit rating.) Thus the returns of investment-grade municipal bonds are determined mostly by changes in interest rates—systematic risk

that cannot be diversified away. Thus there is only a limited benefit from diversifying the risk of default when investing in very-high-credit-quality municipal bonds. However, even the limited benefit should not be ignored. Unless an investor is going to purchase ten or more individual bonds from different issuers, thereby diversifying credit risk, tax-exempt municipal bond funds do provide the important benefit of diversification.

• As with all bonds, the lower the credit quality of a municipal bond, the more crucial the need for diversification becomes. Thus investors considering buying bonds with a credit rating of less than AA should use a low-cost mutual fund.

Secondary Market

• The secondary market for most municipal bonds is an illiquid one; it is characterized by a wide spread between bid and offer prices, particularly at the retail level. Pricing is also opaque, making it difficult for investors to evaluate the price they receive relative to the price in the wholesale market. The implication is that, in general, investors who purchase individual bonds in the retail market should only buy in the primary (initial offering) market where all investors receive the same price, and only if the intent is to buy and hold. On the other hand, investors with access to the wholesale market may, in fact, be able to receive higher yields by buying in the secondary market.

• In the secondary market for municipal bonds, whether buying or selling, larger trades receive better pricing. This has implications for investors deciding between mutual funds and individual bonds.

- Markups and markdowns of 1 to 3 percent are typical in the retail market. However, markups of 3 to 5 percent are not uncommon, and even wider spreads occur far too often.

Passive versus Active Management

- Because all municipal bonds from the same state, with the same high credit rating and same maturity, are highly likely to produce the same return, there is virtually no ability to add value by security selection. In addition, there is no evidence of the ability to forecast interest rates. Thus we can conclude that active management is likely to be a loser's game because of the greater expenses incurred in the effort.
- When it comes to mutual funds, past performance cannot be used to predict future performance. Actively managed funds do not, on average, provide value added in terms of returns. The major cause of underperformance is expenses. There is a consistent one-for-one negative relationship between expense ratios and net returns. Thus investors accessing the municipal bond market through mutual funds should buy the fund that has the lowest expense ratio among the funds that have the desired maturity and credit characteristics.

Having completed our review of the material previously covered, we will address other important issues. We begin with a discussion of the characteristics of the municipal bond market that make it unique and differentiate it from the Treasury and corporate bond markets.

Differentiating Characteristics of the Municipal Bond Markets

One of the main differentiating characteristics of the municipal bond market is that there are fewer participants than in the taxable bond market. For example, while international investors are a significant part of the taxable market, they play no role in the tax-exempt market. This insulates the municipal bond market from the volatility that can be created by "hot money" flows. For example U.S. Treasury securities, being viewed as the safest instruments in the world from a credit perspective, are generally the main beneficiary of capital inflows during "flights to quality" that can occur during a financial or political crisis. Corporate bonds, on the other hand, might be subject to outflows at the same time. Of course, rapid inflows and outflows tend to reverse just as quickly when the crisis is resolved. The absence of these participants from the municipal bond market makes it less volatile than the taxable bond market.

A second difference is that there are no large institutional tax-exempt investors (e.g., pension and profit-sharing plans) in the municipal bond market. Their tax-exempt status makes the purchase of municipal bonds unnecessary. Thus the municipal bond market is not subject to speculative trades as investors shift assets between market segments in an attempt to outperform their benchmarks. For example, if pension fund managers believed that the economic outlook was likely to improve, and thus the risk of corporations defaulting on their bonds would decrease, they might sell Treasury bonds and purchase corporate bonds. If they thought the economic outlook was going to deteriorate and default risk would rise, they would sell corporate bonds and buy Treasuries. Fund managers also shift assets between the various other segments of the taxable bond market (e.g., MBS, emerging-market bonds). The absence of these participants results in lower volatility.

Another factor in the lower volatility of municipal bonds is that it is illegal to short a municipal bond. Going short involves borrowing a security and immediately selling it. The seller expects to eventually purchase the security at a lower price and then return it to the lender. Going short entails the taking of much greater risk than does the ownership of a security. When you own a security your losses are limited to the amount of the purchase. With a short sale losses are unlimited. Thus the practice of selling short is generally limited to speculators (e.g., hedge funds) and traders. Since these investors generally have very high turnover rates, their absence is a third reason why the municipal bond market is less volatile than it is for Treasury or corporate bonds.

Another factor impacting the pricing of municipal bonds is that there is a greater supply of long-term bonds from issuers than there is demand for long-term municipal securities from investors. As we discussed in chapter 4, municipalities are generally trying to match their liabilities with the long-term nature of their assets (e.g., highways, bridges, buildings, parks). On the other hand, most investors demand securities with short to intermediate maturities. In order for the market to absorb all the supply, prices adjust downward (yields rise). This supply-demand imbalance is one of the factors that results in the municipal bond yield curve being steeper than it is for Treasury bonds. There are, however, other factors. First, municipal bonds entail credit risk that increases with time. Second, municipal bonds carry the risk of a change in the tax law that could result in the loss of their tax-exempt status. Third, tax-exempt investors (who buy only taxable securities) such as pension plans and foundations need to buy longer-maturity bonds in order to match their long-term liabilities. This demand puts downward pressure on yields for long-term taxable bonds. There is no such effect in the world of municipal bonds. Thus the "sweet spot" on the municipal bond yield curve is generally farther out than it is for Treasury and corporate securities.

We now turn to a discussion of issues related to the taxation of municipal bonds.

Taxes

Alternative Minimum Tax

While the interest on municipal bonds is generally exempt from federal taxation, there are exceptions. The first is the aforementioned rule that applies to interest on bonds that are bought at a significant discount to par: Unless subject to the de minimis rule, the amount of the discount is subject to ordinary income taxes. The second is the AMT that applies to interest on what are called private activity bonds (PABs). PABs are issued for the purpose of providing special financing benefits for qualified projects such as airports, housing, or industrial development. Interest on all PABs issued after August 7, 1986 must be included in the calculation of the AMT.

The calculation of the income tax for individuals must be done on a parallel tax system. The tax due for individuals is the *greater* of the tax due under regular tax rates or the tax due under the lower tax rate of the AMT. The AMT is designed to prevent taxpayers from avoiding significant tax liability by taking advantage of exclusions from gross income and certain deductions. One of the tax preferences that must be added back into income in terms of calculating the AMT is the interest income from PABs. For those who are subject to the AMT, the value of the tax-exempt feature is thus reduced. Because of this feature, PABs generally carry slightly higher interest rates. The higher rates make PABs attractive to investors not subject to the AMT. This increases the demand for such bonds. The result is that the incremental yield (historically about ten to fifteen basis points, though it can be greater) is not sufficient to offset the loss of the tax benefit for investors subject to the AMT. Thus it is crucial that investors check before purchasing any municipal bond whether they themselves are subject to the AMT and whether the interest on the bond is subject to the AMT.

There are two other important points for investors to be aware of related to the AMT. The first is that mutual funds are the largest buyer of PABs. The attraction is the higher yield—which they advertise in an attempt to attract investors. Investors subject to the AMT may be attracted by the higher *gross* yield. Unfortunately, they may be unaware that the after-tax return may actually be lower than could be achieved by a fund that had a lower gross yield (because none, or a lower percentage, of its bonds are subject to the AMT). The following example will illustrate this point.

Consider two municipal bond funds. Fund A and Fund B both buy securities of the same maturity and credit risk. The only difference between the funds is that Fund A buys no bond that is subject to the AMT. Its average yield is 5 percent, and thus its after-tax return is also 5 percent. Now consider Fund B. Fund B invests 20 percent of its assets in bonds that are subject to the AMT. These bonds yield 5.3 percent, or 0.3 percent more than non-AMT bonds. The remaining 80 percent of its assets are yielding the same 5 percent as the bonds in Fund A. Thus the average yield of Fund B is 5.06 percent (80 percent × 5 percent plus 20 percent × 5.3 percent, which equals 4 percent plus 1.06 percent). Thus Fund B looks to be the more attractive fund as it provides a 0.06 percent greater yield than does Fund A. And it is for investors not subject to the AMT. The problem for investors who are subject to the AMT is that the 5.06 is a gross return, not a net return. Assuming an AMT rate of 28 percent, the net return to investors subject to this tax will only be 4.76 percent. The calculation is as follows. The 80 percent of the portfolio that is not subject to the AMT yields 5 percent, contributing 4 percent (80 percent × 5 percent) to the total return of the portfolio. The net return of the remaining 20 percent that is subject to the AMT is just 0.76 percent (20 percent × 5.3 percent × [1 − 0.28]). Thus Fund A is clearly the superior choice for investors subject to the AMT.

Investors considering the purchase of a municipal bond fund should carefully review the prospectus, which must disclose whether the fund can purchase bonds subject to the AMT, and what, if any, limitations there may be (e.g., a maximum percentage).

There is a second issue related to investors in AMT bonds. While the first issue relates to investors who use mutual funds, this one relates to investors who purchase individual bonds. The secondary market for AMT bonds is less liquid than it is for non-AMT bonds. The result is that if investors need to liquidate a bond prior to maturity (or wish to do so in order to harvest a loss for tax purposes) then they are likely to find that the bids for their bond will be lower than they would have been otherwise. The price difference is likely to reflect a yield differential of perhaps five basis points.

The AMT is an important issue for two reasons. The first is that historically about 10 percent of all municipal bond issues have been subject to the AMT. The second is that because income subject to the AMT is not subject to an inflation adjustment (unless Congress changes the law), more and more taxpayers will become subject to the AMT. Given that it is likely that more and more investors will become subject to the AMT, the price differential between AMT and non-AMT bonds is likely to widen, with negative implications for current holders.

There is one other tax related issue we need to cover.

Deductibility of Interest Expense

In general, interest expense on funds that are borrowed to purchase investment securities is tax deductible. The exception is that any interest expense incurred to *purchase* or *hold* securities, the interest on which is exempt from taxation, is not tax deductible.

In the same spirit, some investors who use investment advisors may take a miscellaneous deduction for advisory fees. However, the amount of the fees that can be attributed to the advice given with regard to municipal bonds is not deductible.

We will now cover issues related to the credit risk of municipal bonds.

Credit Risk

There are two types of municipal bonds, general obligation bonds (GOs) and revenue bonds. General obligation bonds are backed by the full faith, credit, and taxing power of the issuer. The credit worthiness of revenue bonds, on the other hand, is determined by the success of the particular project (e.g., hospital, road, water system). The credit support difference between the two bonds, unfortunately, leads to the great misperception that GOs are safer than revenue bonds. The supposed safety of GOs comes from the phrase "full faith and credit" and the *theoretically* unlimited taxing authority of the issuer. This is in contrast to revenue bonds that get their only support from the revenues generated by the project.

If, in reality, all GOs were safer than all revenue bonds, all GO bonds backed by the full faith and credit of the issuer would be AAA-rated. But this is not the case. The reason this is not true is that in the real world the power to tax is limited. For example, the ability to tax may be limited by state constitution. It can also be limited by economic conditions or even the general mood of the public. Thus the credit rating of a GO will depend on such issues as the strength of the issuer's tax base, the strength and diversity of the economy of the issuer, the total level of outstanding debt of the issuer and its debt coverage ratio (ratio of revenue to debt), and the issuer's historic commitment to prudent fiscal policy.

The ratings of revenue bonds will be based on the issuer's ability to generate revenues sufficient to cover both operating expenses and interest. The stability of revenue will play a major role in determining the rating. In addition, other factors, such as the dependence on governmental support or reimbursement can play significant roles in determining the creditworthiness of a project.

As was mentioned in the review at the beginning of this chapter, municipal bonds have significantly less credit risk than do similarly rated corporate bonds. For example, Standard & Poor's found that over a fifteen-year period a single-A-rated municipal bond was one-tenth as likely to default (0.16 percent default rate) as was a similarly rated corporate bond (1.8 percent rate of default).[1] And, in general, municipal bonds have experienced many fewer defaults than have corporate bonds. However, there are some *sectors* of the municipal bond market that do not have a good credit history—and thus prudent investors are best served by generally avoiding them. Those sectors are housing, health care, and industrial development. A September 1999 Fitch IBCA study on municipal bond default risk found that 7.52 percent of all industrial development bonds issued between 1979 and 1994 had defaulted by 1999. For multifamily housing bonds the number was 4.78 percent, for health care 1.60 percent, and for electric power, 1.46 percent. Contrast these default rates with the following ones: 0.05 percent for water and sewer revenue, 0.04 percent for education (school districts and the like), and 0.01 percent for transportation (highways, public transportation systems). There are two reasons that go a long way toward explaining the high default rates in these areas. The first is that hospitals have a strong dependence on government reimbursement programs that often do not fully cover costs. The second is that many development projects (especially nursing homes) are built as speculative projects by private businesses.

As the municipal bond market is one of the largest markets in the world, there is little reason for a prudent investor to even consider the purchase of bonds from sectors that have experienced such high rates of default.

Credit Enhancements

There are many municipal issues that do not qualify for a high investment rating of AAA or AA. Their lower credit quality has a direct impact on the cost of borrowing. There is, however, also a secondary, indirect effect. Since the demand for municipal bonds is strongest for those in the highest investment grades, a lower credit rating limits the number of potential buyers. This negatively impacts the liquidity of lower-rated bonds, with a corresponding negative impact on interest costs. In order to minimize total costs, the issuer can purchase a credit enhancement, typically in the form of insurance. The cost of insurance to the issuer has historically been in the range of ten to forty basis points per annum—though it can be much greater for highly risky credits.

Weaker credits are not the only ones that can benefit from the purchase of a credit enhancement. Government entities from smaller communities that do not come to market frequently are likely to suffer a liquidity premium. The reason for this liquidity premium is these issuers are neither widely known to the market nor are they likely to bring to market a large enough issue to create sufficient liquidity on a stand-alone basis. For a smaller municipal issuer, buying insurance may even be simpler and less expensive than applying for a credit rating from the major rating agencies. A third type of issuer might also consider buying insurance. When a transaction is very complex, the market for that issue will be negatively impacted. Many potential investors might not even want to consider evaluating the risks. Thus issuers of securities with complex features may find it advantageous to purchase insurance in order to achieve broader market acceptance.

A municipal bond insurance policy may result in significant interest cost savings that are attributable to the higher bond rating as well as the enhanced liquidity of insured bonds. The benefits of insurance are so great that about 50 percent of all newly issued bonds each year are insured.

The municipal bond insurance industry is dominated by the four leading insurers, each with approximately a 25 percent share of the market: AMBAC Assurance Corporation, Financial Guaranty Insurance Company, Financial Security Assurance Inc., and MBIA Insurance Corporation. They are all AAA-rated insurers. All municipal bond insurers are *monoline* insurance companies— they can only insure municipal bonds and are thus not exposed to risks to which property and casualty insurers are exposed. They are also highly regulated by state insurance departments.

The insurance policies written by municipal bond insurers

guarantee that interest and principal will be paid *as scheduled* if the issuer defaults. Each guarantee is unconditional and irrevocable and covers 100 percent of the interest and principal for the entire term of the issue. The risks covered *may* include natural disasters (e.g., earthquakes, floods, hurricanes) and environmental hazards. In the event of default, the insurer would step in to make *timely* (not immediate) payments. Insurance provides value to the investor in several ways:

Safety: A secondary source will meet the issuer's obligations in the event it cannot. Of special interest to investors is that insured bonds have performed better than comparable uninsured bonds during difficult economic times.

Liquidity: Bonds carrying AAA-rated insurance have greater liquidity. Greater liquidity results in lower trading costs. This is important for investors who may need to sell prior to maturity in order to raise capital or may have a need to sell in order to harvest a tax loss at some point.

Note that the market does not consider a bond that receives its AAA rating based on the purchase of insurance to be as strong a credit as a bond that is a *natural* AAA credit. This reflects the market's perception that the monoline insurance companies are not as creditworthy as those issuers that earn a AAA rating on their own. Thus, insured AAA bonds generally carry slightly higher yields than do natural AAAs. The incremental yield might be in the neighborhood of five to ten basis points for short to intermediate maturities and a bit more for longer maturities. In fact, insured AAAs generally trade even a bit cheaper (higher yield) than do natural AAs (perhaps two to four basis points higher yield).

In summary, buying insured bonds can be part of a prudent investment strategy. Investors, however, are best served by *not* relying solely on the credit rating of the issuer (most insured bonds carry a dual rating from the rating agencies—a rating without the insurance and a rating with it). They should also diversify credit risk across both issuers and insurers. Keep in mind that the municipal bond insurance industry has only been in existence since the early 1970s, and thus its claims-paying ability has not been stress-tested by a severe economic condition such as a depression.

In addition to insurance, there are two other types of credit enhancements that issuers can purchase, a letter of credit (LOC) and a line of credit.

Letter of Credit

Letters of credit are irrevocable commitments, typically issued by commercial banks, for a limited period of time (subject to renewal), that allow trustees or fiscal agents to draw on the letters when necessary to make payments of principal or interest on bonds. LOCs present two problems for investors. The first is that they are typically issued for a maximum of ten years (with no guarantee of renewal). Thus there is the obvious potential for a problem to arise if the maturity of the bond purchased extends beyond the term of the LOC. The second problem is that the financial institutions providing the LOCs are generally not as highly rated as the monoline insurers.

Line of Credit

The least valuable form of enhancement is a line of credit or other "backup" credit facility. These are even less valuable than LOCs as conditions usually exist for the provider to not have to advance funds. They are also generally short-term in nature. Investors would best serve themselves by avoiding issues that have their credit enhanced by a line of credit.

There is an additional way in which municipal bonds can have their credit rating enhanced. The enhancement comes as an indirect benefit of pre-refunding a bond.

Pre-refunded Bonds

Consider the following situation. In 2000 a municipality issues a $10 million bond with a 5 percent coupon that will mature in 2030. The bond has its first call date in 2010, with the call option at par. By 2005 interest rates have fallen, and a new issue with a maturity date of 2030 is yielding just 3 percent. If the municipality waits until 2010 to call the bond and take advantage of lower rates, rates by then might have once again risen. In order to avoid this risk, and take advantage of the current low-rate environment, the municipality issues a new $10 million bond with a maturity of 2030 (or perhaps even longer). It uses the proceeds to buy U.S. Treasury securities with a maturity of 2010 (matching the call date). The issuer then places the Treasury securities in an irrevocable trust. The trust uses the interest it receives to pay the interest on the older debt and the principal it receives to redeem the older, higher-yielding bonds at the 2010 call date. This process is called *defeasance*. The benefit to the issuer is that they will save on interest costs from the call date to the final maturity of the original issue.

Pre-refunded bonds can provide investors with the highest possible credit quality because payment is no longer dependent upon the revenue stream or tax collections of the issuer. Instead, payment is guaranteed by the collateral (generally a special type of

U.S. Treasury instrument). Therefore, pre-refunded bonds, at least those that are backed by U.S. Treasury securities, are rated AAA.

Bonds are generally pre-refunded in low-interest-rate environments. Therefore, they are usually priced at premiums to par value. Because many investors avoid premium bonds, at the time of the pre-refunding these bonds will generally trade at a greater yield to maturity than par or discount bonds of comparable quality. This "market inefficiency" is a free lunch (and there are not many of those in the world of investing) for those willing to purchase premium bonds with calls that have been waived by the issuer. Another benefit of premium bonds is that they provide greater price stability because their higher coupon rates generate higher cash flows than current coupon or lower coupon bonds, thus cushioning the impact of rising interest rates.

It is worth noting that investors in the original bond receive a permanent benefit when a bond is pre-refunded. The reason is that, for all practical purposes, the original issue is now a tax-exempt bond backed by the U.S. Treasury. The increase in the credit quality from the escrow of U.S. Treasury securities provides a benefit in terms of market price. The market recognizes the impeccable quality of the credit and, therefore, pre-refunded municipals typically trade with a yield five to ten basis points lower than non-pre-refunded AAA-rated municipals. A point of note is that most municipal bonds are issued with first call dates of no more than ten years. Therefore, almost all bonds pre-refunded to a call date fall within ten years of maturity.

In summary, pre-refunded bonds can play an important role in a municipal bond portfolio. And as long as all calls are waived prior to the refunding date, investors should not be concerned by the premium at which they trade. In fact, as mentioned above, the premium provides a defensive feature. In addition, the bonds are of the highest quality, and they will generally fall within the part of the yield curve investors are trying to access.

Short-Term Municipal Securities

In chapter 6, "The World of Short-Term Fixed-Income Securities," we learned that there are both taxable money-market funds and municipal money-market funds that investors can use for liquidity, as opposed to investment, purposes. We also learned how to determine which provides the highest after-tax return.

While money-market funds are the most common instrument used for saving (i.e., emergency funds and funds needed for liquidity purposes) because of their convenience and safety, two municipal bond security types—*municipal auction rate securities* (MARS) and *variable rate demand obligations* (VRDOs)—can serve a comparable purpose while adding more value via higher yields.

MARS and VRDOs

While these securities are actually long-term bonds, they have many features that make them similar to money-market funds or other very short-term instruments. For example, in terms of liquidity, some of these bonds offer daily, weekly, or monthly reset schedules—dates when the interest rate on the bond is set. The result it that even though a bond may mature in 2035, it can have a daily, weekly, or monthly interest pay date and an optional redemption provision that allows investors to redeem their principal at par on any of the interest pay dates. Because of the feature of *par in and par out* liquidity on a very short-term basis there are usually no concerns regarding loss of principal.

Another positive feature is that many of these instruments carry the desired high credit rating. For example, the credit ratings of most MARS range from AAA to A. Because of the unique structure of these bonds, both MARS and VRDOs are commonly assigned both a long-term and a short-term rating. However, if an investor purchases MARS or VRDOs as a substitute for a money-market fund—and thus does not plan to hold the bonds to maturity—he might only need to concentrate on the bond's short-term rating.

The conclusion we can draw is that MARS and VRDOs have features that make them similar to money-market funds in terms of both liquidity and safety of principal. And the attraction is that they provide a higher yield than tax-exempt money-market funds. In addition, there have even been times when, despite their tax-exempt status, they have provided higher yields than *taxable* money-market funds. For example, a taxable Schwab money-market fund offered a seven-day current yield of 0.78 percent (as of June 30, 2004).[2] A VRDO with a maturity date of 2040 had a rate of 1.03 percent (as of July 1, 2004).[3]

There are several reasons why these instruments are able to provide higher returns. The main reason is that money-market funds have expenses; an operating expense ratio of 0.5 to 0.7 percent is fairly common. A second reason is the very large minimum purchase requirement. MARS and VRDOs generally require a minimum investment of $100,000. Thus the issuer has lower costs in managing a program. A third reason is that these instruments do not come with the check-writing privileges of many money-market funds (again reducing costs).

MARS and VRDOs also have a disadvantage relative to money-market funds in that transactions costs are likely to be charged by the custodian when buying and selling these securities. Thus the benefits of the greater yield must be weighed against the incremental costs and the lack of convenience.

Summary

Both MARS and VRDOs provide high credit ratings, high liquidity, and higher yields relative to comparable investment vehicles such as municipal money-market funds. This combination makes them attractive low-risk alternatives for those investors who can meet the minimum-purchase requirement.

Other Short-Term Municipal Securities

Investors who do not have the liquidity needs of a tax-exempt money-market account, but still desire to keep maturities short, have a wide variety of securities to choose from.

Bond Anticipation Note (BAN): Short-term loan repaid from the proceeds of a future bond issue.

Tax Anticipation Note (TAN): Short-term loan to be repaid from future tax collections.

Revenue Anticipation Note (RAN): Short-term loan to be repaid from future revenues, either general revenues or project-specific revenues.

Tax and Revenue Anticipation Note (TRAN): Short-term loan to be repaid from future taxes or other revenue sources.

Grant Anticipation Note (GAN): Short-term loan to be repaid from an intergovernmental grant to be received in the future.

The following are the common characteristics of these short-term instruments:

- Initial maturities are less than thirteen months.
- Most are sold at a discount to par and mature at par. (They do not pay coupon interest.)

Because the demand for these securities is very high, depending on the investor's tax bracket, at times they might actually provide lower after-tax returns than comparable taxable instruments. Thus, as is always the case, investors should compare returns of taxable and tax-exempt securities before investing.

Before completing our discussion on municipal bonds we need to cover one more type of security—a *taxable* municipal bond.

Taxable Municipal Bonds

A taxable municipal bond is not an oxymoron. There are municipal bonds that are taxable. Taxable munis are bonds that are issued by the same entities that issue tax-exempt securities. The bonds, however, are deemed to be issued for a private purpose (not for the public good). A good example might be a bond issued to finance a sports facility. The yields on taxable munis are comparable to those issued by taxable corporate bonds. Thus they might be worth considering for tax-exempt or tax-deferred accounts, or for investors in the lowest tax brackets.

We have now completed the section on municipal bonds. The next chapter will cover issues related to developing a fixed-income portfolio, including the development of an investment policy statement.

CHAPTER ELEVEN

◆

How to Design and Construct Your Fixed-Income Portfolio

In investment management, the real opportunity to achieve superior results is not in scrambling to outperform the market, but in establishing and adhering to appropriate investment policies over the long term—policies that position the portfolio to benefit from riding with the main long-term forces in the market. —Charles Ellis, *Investment Policy*

Success in investing doesn't correlate with IQ. Once you have ordinary intelligence, what you need is the temperament to control the urges that get other people in trouble. Investing. —Warren Buffett

Good fortune is what happens when opportunity meets with planning. —Thomas Edison

Napoleon, perhaps the world's greatest general, provided the following insight: "Most battles are won or lost [in the preparation stage] long before the first shot is fired." Similarly, investment success is likely to be determined long before the first investment is made. As you have learned, the first ingredient for a successful investment experience is an understanding of how markets work. That knowledge leads to the determination of the winning strategy. However, a winning strategy is a necessary, though not a sufficient, condition for success. The sufficient condition is to be able to implement that strategy in the most effective manner. The most brilliant military strategy can fail if either the tactics used to implement the strategy are flawed or the execution of the tactics is mismanaged. Similarly, the choice of inefficient investment vehicles can undermine the best investment strategy. And poor execution of even a well-thought-out plan will lead to less than optimal results.

This chapter begins with a discussion on the issue of which investment vehicles are the preferred choice as building blocks of a fixed-income portfolio. We will then discuss the tactical issues of building a laddered portfolio, the best location in which to hold fixed-income assets, and fixed-income investing in retirement. The chapter concludes with directions on how to build your own investment policy statement.

Individual Securities or
Mutual Funds and ETFs?

Once an investor has decided on the appropriate asset allocation for his or her portfolio, a decision must be made about the best way to implement the plan. The investor has a choice of buying individual securities, mutual funds, or exchange-traded funds (ETFs). These investment choices are like the products you find in the hair-care aisle at the supermarket. There are dozens of shampoos available, any one of which could be the best product depending on whether you have dry hair, thin hair, need dandruff control, or like the convenience of a 2-in-1 shampoo and conditioner. Clearly choosing the right product is based on personal needs—for you there may be only one right choice. Similarly, when it comes to the world of investing there is no one right answer. Mutual funds and ETFs often provide benefits over individual holdings, but those benefits may not outweigh the costs. The right answer will depend on a variety of issues that might be unique to each investor, or they might be unique to the asset class to which the investor seeks exposure. Looking at the benefits of each strategy will allow you to find the best solution given your personal situation.

Mutual funds and ETFs offer many benefits, with the most significant being convenience and diversification.

Convenience

Unless the mutual fund is a load fund (which should be avoided), investors can buy and sell shares, if the transaction is made directly with the fund sponsor, at the net asset value (there is no bid-offer spread; buying and selling is done at the same price), and can generally do so without incurring any transactions costs. If the transaction is made through a brokerage firm, a relatively small fee will generally (though not always) be incurred. This feature allows investors to invest small amounts over time in a cost-effective manner. It also allows for ease in the reinvestment of interest.

ETFs, on the other hand, do not trade at the NAV. Thus there is not only a transaction cost involved in the form of a sales commission, but the investor must also absorb the cost of the price difference between the bid and the offer.

The issue of investing small amounts is an important one when it comes to municipal and corporate bonds. The reason is that larger blocks receive better pricing (which is not the case with equities). Buying or selling relatively small amounts of a municipal or corporate bond will generally lead to a large markup or markdown being incurred. This renders such transactions cost prohibitive.

Diversification

Another very significant benefit of mutual funds (and ETFs) is that they allow investors to achieve broad diversification across an asset class to which they seek exposure. Broad diversification is critical when the performance of a single security within the asset class has a relatively low correlation with the performance of the asset class itself. This is certainly the case with stocks. The performance of any one stock within the S&P 500 Index might be dramatically different than the performance of the index itself. The only way to ensure that you earn the return of the asset class is to own the entire asset class.

There is a great deal of academic research on the subject of how much diversification is needed to keep what is known as tracking error to an acceptable level. In this case, tracking error refers to the variance between the performance of the entire asset class and the performance of a subset of the asset class. Research has found that to keep tracking error to an expected level of 5 percent (a level many investors would likely find unacceptably large), an investor would have to own approximately one hundred different individual stocks from one specific asset class. Thus building a portfolio that is globally diversified across perhaps eight to ten equity asset classes would be well beyond the resources of almost all individual investors. Thus mutual funds are the preferred choice when it comes to *equities*. The issue of diversification is quite different when we come to the world of fixed-income securities. Let's see why this is the case.

To begin with, investors who limit their holdings to Treasury securities have no need whatsoever to diversify credit risk. And investors can ensure themselves of wholesale prices by buying and selling via the TreasuryDirect program. In addition, there is a great deal of transparency of pricing of Treasury securities since prices are available on at least a daily basis in financial publications such as the *Wall Street Journal*. This helps keep pricing "honest." Thus, in general, the only value a fund might add (since there is no evidence that managers are likely to add value by correctly forecasting interest rates and adjusting maturities accordingly) is convenience. Fortunately, that convenience can be purchased relatively cheaply through low-cost vehicles like those offered by Vanguard or ETFs. Is the price worth the convenience? That is an individual decision.

Once we move beyond the world of Treasuries the benefits of diversification that a mutual fund can bring begin to increase. In order to evaluate the benefits of diversification, we need to understand the source of most of the returns of fixed-income assets.

Because most of the returns of high-credit-quality fixed-income securities are derived from interest rate risk (which is the same for all securities), the benefits of, and thus the need for, diversification are substantially reduced. As was stated above, with U.S. Treasury debt the need for diversification is nonexistent—100 percent of the risk is systematic risk (interest rate risk) that cannot be diversified away (there is no credit risk to diversify away).

As we move to bonds of the highest investment grades (specifically the securities of the U.S. agencies and the government-sponsored entities) the need for diversification doesn't change that much because there is very little credit risk. Even as we move to other AAA-rated bonds, especially AAA-rated municipal bonds, the need for diversification doesn't change much. Think of it this way, bonds of the highest investment grades are commodities. In other words, taxable bonds of the same maturity and same high credit quality are good substitutes for each other. For municipal bonds we would have to add that to be a good substitute for each other they would have to be from the same state as well.

The result is that while it would not be prudent to build a portfolio by selecting a small sample of stocks from one asset class, prudent diversification can be accomplished with a relatively small sample of high-credit-quality bonds. The reason is that you can have a high degree of confidence that the relatively small sample will produce very similar returns to that produced by the entire population of similarly rated bonds of the same maturity. And the higher the credit quality, the more confident you can be, and the less important diversification becomes. Conversely, the lower the credit quality, the more important the need for diversification of fixed-income assets becomes. For example, high-yield bonds are not good substitutes for one another—two high-yield bonds are far less likely to provide similar returns than are two AAA-rated bonds. Thus if an investor sought the higher expected returns that high-yield bonds provide, they should do so through a mutual fund that might own one hundred different bonds, and not through the purchase of individual bonds.

The conclusion we can draw is that if an investor limits herself to bonds of the highest quality and has a portfolio of perhaps $500,000, she could consider building her own portfolio, saving the costs of a mutual fund or ETF. A $500,000 portfolio would allow her to purchase securities in large enough blocks that she could limit the markups and markdowns to acceptable levels, and she could diversify the credit risk across perhaps as many as ten issuers. Owning that number of securities would also allow her to diversify the term risk. This could be accomplished by perhaps buying ten bonds, one maturing in each of the next ten years.

Size Matters

Another benefit of owning bonds through a mutual fund is that a fund (or ETF), because it buys and sells large blocks, is able to minimize markups and markdowns, thus minimizing trading costs. It is unlikely that individuals acting on their own will be able to obtain institutional prices. Thus even do-it-yourself investors with a $500,000 or larger portfolio should limit themselves to buying in the new-issue market, where they can be assured that they are getting institutional pricing. They should also only buy individual bonds if they are virtually certain that they will be able to hold the bonds to maturity. The issue of trading costs could easily more than offset the expense ratio of a fund if an investor attempted to buy and sell in the secondary market. Individuals should avoid doing so on their own, unless they wish to make their broker rich (not a usual objective).

Advantages of Individual Securities

While owning mutual funds can provide advantages, there are advantages to owning individual bonds. The first, as we have already discussed, is that you avoid the operating expenses of a fund. The second is that for taxable accounts, an investor in mutual funds is only able to harvest tax losses (have Uncle Sam share the pain) at the fund level. An investor owning individual bonds can manage taxes at the individual security level. Thus there will be more opportunities to harvest losses. This is especially important because, unlike equity funds, fixed-income funds do not have it as a stated objective to tax-manage their portfolios (harvesting losses along the way). In addition, mutual funds cannot pass through to investors realized losses that are not offset by gains.

It is essential for investors to keep in mind that with Treasury bonds, where pricing is transparent, and you can deal directly with the Treasury, the trading costs of tax-loss harvesting would be low. However, when it comes to municipal and corporate bonds, investors trying to trade on their own would probably find that any tax benefit from harvesting losses would likely be offset by the bid-offer spread and the dealer markdowns that would be incurred when harvesting the losses, and the potential markup paid on the repurchase of a similar bond (unless the investor waited until a new issue was available).

Another benefit of owning individual securities is that investors can take 100 percent control over the credit risk and the term risk of their portfolios. This is generally not the case with mutual funds. They can also take control over the timing of cash flows from such a portfolio. This is particularly important to investors relying on their fixed-income assets to provide the cash flow they need to maintain their desired lifestyle.

There is another benefit of owning individual securities. With a mutual fund, after a period of falling interest rates, "hot money" chasing recent performance will typically buy into the fund. The fund, therefore, must buy more bonds in a low-rate environment. Then if rates begin to rise, the hot money will leave, forcing the fund (and long-term investors in the fund) to suffer capital losses that can't be "waited out." On the other hand, an investor owning individual bonds, who is satisfied with the YTM when the bond was purchased, is not subject to the same problem (other investors cannot force him to sell at depressed prices).

Separate Account Managers

Fortunately, for individual investors wishing to take advantage of the benefits of owning individual securities, at least for those with portfolios of sufficient size, they don't have to go it alone. They can utilize a separate account manager. A separate account manager builds a portfolio of individual securities that is tailored to the specific needs of the investor. The value of a separate account manager is that the investor receives the benefits of owning individual securities (ability to tailor the portfolio in terms of credit risk, term risk, tax manage [harvest losses] at the individual security level, and minimize state and local taxes), without having to pay retail prices on transactions. The separate account manager should have access to the wholesale markets. And the separate account manager should be managing a large amount of assets in order to be able to provide the maximum benefit to individual investors.

One benefit is that a separate account manager is able to aggregate the purchases of different individual investors seeking to buy similar bonds. The following example will illustrate how investors can benefit from this process. A broker-dealer might offer to sell a block of $50,000 of a particular municipal or corporate bond at a price of 102. However, if the trade was for a block of $250,000 the offer might be just 101.75. And for $500,000 the price might be 101.5. Thus a firm that could aggregate five different purchases for $100,000 would be able to save each investor one-half of one percent on the trade (the difference in price between 101.5 and 102). As long as each buyer was willing to be somewhat patient, so that a "group" could be put together, each buyer will benefit from the aggregation process.

Another benefit of working with a separate account manager is that the manager may be able to perform tax-loss harvesting without incurring large trading costs. Again, an example will illustrate the importance of working with a separate account manager who is managing a large amount of assets. Let's assume that a separate account manager has two clients who both live in the state of California. Each owns a $100,000 AAA-rated California municipal bond of similar maturity but from different issuers. Let's also assume rates have risen significantly since the original purchases were made. Both investors would like to be able to harvest losses, but the trading costs would be high. The manager-advisor would simply contact a broker-dealer and ask it to cross two trades. Investor A buys the bond of investor B, and investor B buys investor A's bond. The term "cross" implies that A's sale and B's purchase of the same bond are done at the same price, and A's purchase and B's sale of the same bond are also done at the same price, with no markup or markdown. The prices at which the cross trades are made are determined by the broker-dealer. Because the broker-dealer takes no risk in the transaction, it is willing to perform the service for a relatively low fee, perhaps $50-75. This is only possible if the manager-advisor firm has a large enough client base to make cross trades of similar securities possible.

A good way to access a separate account manager is through a fee-only registered investment advisor (RIA) firm that provides such services. There are a small number of fee-only RIAs that provide investors with access to the wholesale markets. Our firm, for example, has a very experienced team of fixed-income specialists that helps investors build portfolios of individual securities. The team shops for prices among about thirty dealers in an effort to obtain the best possible price. And because it is not a broker-dealer itself, the investor can be sure that no spread has been added to the price the firm obtained from the broker-dealer. This is a distinguishing point because there are some separate account managers that are also broker-dealers who in managing an account will charge a fee and mark up the bonds as well.

Of course, although a fee-only RIA will add no markups or markdowns to the price, those services are not free. The investor will be paying for the value of the advice, typically as an annual percentage of the total assets under management. However, helping to offset the costs is that the investor avoids the fees of a mutual fund or a separate account money manager (who typically will charge a significantly higher fee than Vanguard charges for its fixed-income mutual funds). The value added from fixed-income portfolio building (and tax management) services is a significant benefit that an advisory firm can provide.

A good analogy for this type of service from a fee-only RIA is the services of an interior decorator. Interior decorators receive a fee for the value they bring in designing and implementing a plan. The cost of their services can be offset, at least to some degree, as they often enable the retail buyer to purchase furniture and accessories in the wholesale market.

Before concluding, there is one more issue related to owning bond mutual funds (but not ETFs) about which investors should be both aware and concerned.

A Word of Caution

Many bond funds (particularly closed-end funds—funds that trade like stocks) employ the use of leverage in an attempt to increase returns. If they are able to borrow at a lower rate than the returns they earn, the returns of the fund will be enhanced. Of course leverage works both ways. In rising-rate environments the use of leverage can lead to not just lower returns, but to outright losses. The use of leverage turns an investment into more of a speculation, a bet on interest rates. Thus funds that employ leverage should be avoided. Investors can determine whether a fund uses leverage by reading the prospectus.

Summary

As you can see, there is no right answer as to which approach, individual bonds or mutual funds (or ETFs), is the superior approach. The answer will depend on the unique situation of each investor, as well as the preference for convenience versus do-it-yourself control. And finally, high-net-worth investors don't have to settle for choosing between owning mutual funds and individual securities. They can have the best of both worlds by employing the services of a separate account manager, especially one that is also their fee-only investment advisor.

Having completed the section on which vehicles make the best choice for implementing our fixed-income investment strategy, we can move to a discussion on a specific tactic.

Laddering: A Prudent Tactical Approach to Portfolio Construction

As we discussed in chapter 2, there are eight types of risk related to fixed-income investing, one of which is reinvestment risk. Reinvestment risk is the risk that when the security an investor has purchased matures, interest rates will be lower than they were at the time of purchase. Thus when the investor reinvests the proceeds from the maturing instrument she will receive a lower rate of return. Reinvestment risk also applies to the reinvestment of coupon interest. Minimizing price risk comes at the cost of accepting reinvestment risk, and vice versa. Consider the following example.

Let's assume that the current yield curve is flat: All maturities are yielding 4 percent. If we want to limit price risk (perhaps because we are concerned about the potential for interest rates to rise), we can purchase a one-year Treasury. However, having done so, we are accepting the risk that in one year all interest rates will be lower. Thus when we reinvest the proceeds at maturity we will receive a lower rate of return. This might impact our ability to maintain a desired lifestyle. On the other hand, if we extend the maturity to ten years, and interest rates rise dramatically, the value of the longer bonds would fall sharply. As you can see, it is impossible to minimize both price risk and reinvestment risk at the same time.

A prudent solution to achieving a balance between controlling price and reinvestment risk is to create what is called a laddered bond portfolio. Laddering involves building a portfolio of individual bonds with increasingly longer maturities. This could involve buying equal amounts of bonds with maturities of perhaps one through ten years. Or it might involve a ladder with maturities of two, four, six, eight, and ten years. Since buying small lots of individual bonds can increase costs, the number of bonds and thus the number of maturities used might be influenced by the dollars available—the larger the portfolio, the more individual bonds and maturities can be used in constructing the ladder. Let's look at how a simple ladder might work.

An investor with $500,000 in fixed-income assets purchases ten individual bonds of $50,000 each with maturities from one to ten years. The average maturity of the portfolio is 5.5 years. At the end of the first year, the one-year instrument matures and thus the ladder is now for only $450,000 with maturities from one to nine years. The average maturity has fallen from 5.5 to 5 years. In order to maintain the desired balance between price and reinvestment risk the investor needs to again extend the ladder by using the proceeds from the matured instrument to purchase a bond with a maturity of ten years.

Ladders provide the following benefits:

- They allow investors to match maturities to known or desired cash flow needs.

- They allow investors to balance price risk and reinvestment risk.

- They allow investors to avoid the expense of a mutual fund or an active separate account manager.

- There is no active trading. Thus trading expenses are minimized.

- For taxable accounts, loss harvesting can be performed at the individual bond level.

- The income stream stays relatively constant, as only a small portion of the portfolio matures each year.

- Over time, the portfolio will contain bonds purchased in both low and high interest rate environments.

- If interest rates rise, the bonds with longer maturities will likely experience a fall in price. However, when a bond matures and the proceeds are used to once again extend the ladder to the desired length, the investor will benefit from the higher current yields. On the other hand, if interest rates fall, while the proceeds of the maturing bond will have to be reinvested at lower rates, the value of the portfolio will have increased.

As is the case with most investment issues, there is no right answer to how long the ladder should be. The following are issues that should be considered when determining the appropriate length.

- The longer the maturity, the greater the correlation of the fixed-income assets with the equity assets in the portfolio. Thus, while you reduce reinvestment risk when you extend maturity, you increase the price risk of the fixed-income assets and you also increase the risk of the overall portfolio.

- The historical evidence for taxable bonds is that, on average, investors have not been rewarded for extending maturities beyond five years (remember that for municipal bonds the yield curve is typically steeper).

- The best predictor of future yield curves is today's yield curve. Thus investors are likely to achieve the *highest* return by extending maturity until the point where the yield curve is no longer upward sloping.

- While extending maturities as long as the yield curve is positively sloped is likely to produce the greatest return, investors accept more risk by doing so. Thus it seems prudent to establish a rule of thumb that requires a minimum incremental yield for each additional year of maturity as compensation for the incremental risk. For taxable investments a suggested hurdle is twenty basis points per annum, and for municipal bonds a suggested hurdle is fifteen basis points. However, if the yield curve is very flat, or even negatively sloped, this rule of thumb will lead to the creation of a portfolio that is very short-term in nature. The result will be a portfolio with little price risk, but with great reinvestment risk. Thus investors using the laddered approach might want to add a second requirement of having a minimum and maximum weighted-average maturity for the ladder. For example, the minimum weighted-average maturity might be three years and the maximum might be five years.

Summary

In summary, a laddered portfolio is a simple yet prudent approach to fixed-income portfolio design. The shorter maturities balance the price risk of the longer maturities, and the longer maturities balance the reinvestment risk of the shorter maturities. And over time investors will be purchasing bonds in both high- and low-rate environments. Thus laddering a bond portfolio is an effective way to diversify price risk and reinvestment risk. The laddered approach allows investors to meet current income requirements while preserving capital and keeping price and reinvestment risk at acceptable levels. A further benefit is that a laddered approach allows investors to stop worrying about forecasting interest rates, something few if any investors have demonstrated an ability to do successfully. As is the case with investing in general, the key to the success of a laddered portfolio strategy is to have the discipline to ignore the noise of the market, noise that can lead you to abandon your well-thought-out plan.

The next section discusses the very important topic of asset location. Unfortunately, it is another case of the conventional wisdom being wrong.

The Asset Location Decision

Feng shui literally means "wind" and "water." The goal of this ancient Chinese philosophy is to create a harmonious relationship between objects within a home, resulting in equilibrium and good fortune for the homeowner. The rules of feng shui are used to determine the designing and siting of cities, buildings, graves, homes, furniture, and so on. The placement of furniture in a home, for example, determines if there is a favorable flow of energy and thus a favorable environment. Simply put, feng shui is the art of placement, or location. As you will learn, when it comes to investing, while the asset *allocation* decision is the most significant decision an investor makes, the asset *location* decision

202

also plays an important role. The reason is that the asset *location* decision can have a substantial impact on the final wealth created through its impact on after-tax returns, the only kind we get to spend.

The traditional approach to the location decision has been to hold equities, and especially actively managed funds, in tax-deferred accounts and to hold tax-exempt bonds (for investors in all but the lowest tax bracket) in taxable accounts. The arguments for this location decision are that the high turnover rate of actively managed equity funds generally leads to tax inefficiencies caused by the required distribution of realized gains, and that the tax-deferral provides valuable shelter for assets with high expected returns.

A study, "Optimal Asset Location and Allocation with Taxable and Tax-Deferred Investing," concluded that the traditional approach is not likely to prove the most efficient way to create wealth.[1] Instead, the winning strategy is to hold as much equity as possible in taxable accounts and hold taxable fixed-income investments and tax inefficient REITs in tax-deferred accounts. This is especially true now that there are available vehicles in which individuals can invest that are more tax efficient than actively managed funds. First, there are index and passive asset-class funds that are, in general, more tax efficient than actively managed funds due to their lower turnover. Second, there are now passively managed funds that are specifically managed for tax efficiency. Third, there are exchange-traded funds (ETFs) that are also relatively tax efficient.

Even with tax-inefficient actively managed equity funds the study concluded that unless the yield on taxable bonds was below the yield on an actively managed fund, the active equity fund should be held in a taxable account. "Only in the extreme case in which an actively managed fund distributes 100 percent of its capital gains each year, and all gains realized are short term, would the investor be indifferent to holding the actively managed mutual fund or riskless taxable bond in a tax-deferred account."[2]

The authors noted that this location strategy should be followed *unless* the active fund was able to substantially outperform similar tax-efficient equity investments on a risk-adjusted basis. The authors estimated that a *certainty-equivalent* pretax abnormal return (net of all transactions costs and fees) of about sixty-five basis points per annum would be needed to justify holding an actively managed fund in a tax-deferred account and municipal bonds in a taxable account, instead of tax-efficient index funds in a taxable account and taxable bonds in a tax-deferred account. With the average active fund having expenses of well over 1 percent, the required *certainty-equivalent* pretax abnormal gross return is probably on average close to, or even greater than, 2 percent per annum.[3]

Given the substantial body of evidence that the average active fund underperforms, and that there is no way yet known to identify the few future winners ahead of time, the prudent strategy is to hold tax-efficient equity funds in taxable accounts and taxable bonds in the tax-deferred account.

The exception to this asset location strategy is the investor who needs to achieve a rate of return that requires her to hold a very high equity allocation. She, therefore, may need to hold some equities in a tax-deferred account. In this case the least tax-efficient equity holdings (such as REITs or non-tax-managed funds) should be allocated to the tax-deferred account. Alternatively, she may be able to achieve the same expected return with a lower equity allocation but a greater allocation to the higher expected returning asset classes of value and small-cap stocks. This would then allow her to hold more, or even all, of her equities in a taxable account. Since there are available tax-efficient ways to hold these asset classes (either tax-managed funds or ETFs) this alternative strategy should be considered as a more efficient way to achieve the financial objective.

The preference for holding equities in the taxable account is based on:

- Tax-deferred accounts such as IRAs and 401(k)s convert long-term capital gains on equities into ordinary income upon distribution. For most investors the ordinary income tax rate is higher.

- By holding equities in tax-deferred accounts investors lose the potential for a "step-up in basis" upon death. The step-up may totally eliminate capital-gains taxes for the estate.

- Capital-gains taxes are due only when realized. Investors do have at least some ability to time the realization of gains. In addition, the advent of tax-managed funds and ETFs has greatly improved the tax efficiency of equity investing.

- When holding a diversified portfolio of equities or equity mutual funds in a taxable account there may be opportunities to harvest tax losses, producing greater tax efficiency.

- If equities are held in a tax-deferred account the investor loses the ability to donate appreciated shares to charity, thus avoiding capital-gains taxes altogether.

It is essential that investors understand that the above analysis is based on *preference*—when they are going to hold both stocks and fixed-income investments and have a choice of location. Regardless of whether the account will hold stocks or fixed-income investments, investors should always prefer to first fund their deductible retirement accounts (i.e., IRA, 401(k), or 403(b)) or Roth IRA before investing any taxable dollars (except for creating an emergency fund). Because these accounts are the most tax-efficient investment vehicles, investors should take maximum advantage of their ability under the law to fund them. Also, in general, individuals currently in high tax brackets who expect to be in lower tax brackets should prefer the deductible retirement accounts to a Roth IRA, while individuals currently in a low tax bracket should favor the Roth.

Before turning to the discussion on the development of the investment policy statement we have one more issue to discuss: Should investment strategy change as we move from the accumulation phase to the withdrawal phase?

Fixed-Income Investing in Retirement

Early in the book we asked the questions: Are fixed-income assets expected to generate income that is needed to meet living expenses? Or, are fixed-income assets being used to reduce the risks of an equity portfolio? The answer was that for most investors (with the exception of retired individuals), the overriding motivation for including fixed-income assets is usually risk reduction, not achieving the highest expected return. This is generally true, however, only in the accumulation stage of our investment life cycle. During the withdrawal stage, generating the highest expected return from fixed income while maintaining a still acceptable level of risk might take priority over risk reduction. The ability to generate greater income by extending maturity might override concerns that take priority during the accumulation phase (i.e., the increased price volatility of longer maturity assets, their higher correlation with the risks of equity investing, and their increased risk of inflation). For these investors, building a laddered portfolio (e.g., buying bonds of maturities from one to ten years) with a somewhat longer maturity might be the prudent, and possibly even required, approach.

For these investors the basic principles we have discussed should still apply. First, purchase only securities that carry one of the highest investment grades (AA or better). Second, extend maturity only if you are getting paid sufficiently to take the risk. As we discussed in chapter 4, you might consider establishing the following rule: Extend the maturity only if by extending one year you gain at least an incremental yield of twenty basis points for taxable instruments and fifteen basis points for tax-exempt instruments.

Having completed the discussion on tactical issues we can now turn our attention to the development of a formal battle plan.

The Investment Policy Statement

We need to learn to set our course by the stars, not by the lights of every passing ship.
—General Omar Nelson Bradley

What the wise do in the beginning, fools do in the end.
—Warren Buffett

An investment policy statement (IPS) is the road map for investors. It should outline and prescribe the strategy for a prudent and individualized investment philosophy. A written and signed statement is needed because it allows the investor to explicitly articulate a well-thought-out long-term investment policy, setting out the investment management procedures and long-term investment goals. Writing and signing the document is likely to assist in protecting the investor from ad hoc revisions that are caused by emotions generated by the noise of the market—emotions such as greed and envy in bull markets and fear and panic in bear markets. Academic research has found that all too often investors succumb to these emotions, almost invariably to the investor's detriment. A written policy statement helps assure that rational analysis is the primary basis for investment decisions, thus avoiding mistakes caused by emotional decision making. In addition, for investors who believe that they do not have the time, ability, knowledge, discipline, and perhaps even the interest to manage their own portfolio, the prudent strategy would be to delegate that role to an advisor who does. The IPS will be the road map for the advisor to follow.

Despite the importance of the IPS, it is our experience that only a very small percentage of all investors have a written investment plan. Amazingly, virtually none of the investors whom we meet that work with stockbrokers as their investment advisor have a written IPS. Then again, based on our conversations with ex-stockbrokers, over 90 percent of their training relates to sales, not investments. Another explanation for this phenomenon might be that if investors had a well-thought-out plan, then they could not be sold products that don't fit into the plan—and brokers would make less money.

Consider the following question: How can investors without an IPS effectively analyze any investment decision without knowing how it impacts an overall strategy? Of course, they cannot. Perhaps that is one reason that investors who work with stockbrokers generally have such poor results.

To summarize, the IPS can be thought of as a contract with yourself, and your investment advisor, if you choose to work with one. Its purpose is to:

- Establish reasonable expectations, objectives, strategy, and the implementation guidelines for the investment of the portfolio's assets. These should be based on the three branches of the IPS decision tree—the investor's ability, willingness, and need to take risk.

- Set forth an investment structure detailing permitted investments and the desired allocation across asset classes. Arriving at the correct asset allocation is a critical part of the process, as it determines virtually all of the risk and rewards of the investment portfolio. Thus it is essential to get the allocation right.

- Serve as a reference over time to provide long-term discipline for an established plan.

The Fixed-Income IPS

The fixed-income IPS should begin with defining your goals. Before you can decide on what fixed-income investments are appropriate you must decide on whether the main objective of the assets is to generate income or to provide stability of principal. Once that is accomplished, the type of assets should be defined. The next step is to determine the investment horizon. The horizon should be aligned either with the need for cash flow *or* the need to diversify the risks of an equity portfolio (in which case maturities should remain short-term). Decisions must be made as to appropriate maturities. The next step is to set guidelines for acceptable credit ratings.

The following illustrates the issues that a fixed-income IPS should address as well as providing an example. Note that, as we have discussed, there is no one universally correct solution. The policies described here, therefore, are merely examples that may or may not be the same ones you would incorporate into your own IPS.

- *The type of investment vehicles:* Both individual bonds and low-cost and passively managed mutual funds will be used to construct the portfolio.

- *The average maturity:* The average maturity of the portfolio will not exceed five years, but cannot be less than two years.

- *The maximum maturity of any one bond:* The maturity of any one bond cannot exceed ten years.

- *The minimal acceptable credit rating:* The minimal acceptable credit rating is A.

- *The maximum allocation for each credit rating:* Bonds with a credit rating of A cannot exceed 10 percent of the portfolio, and bonds with a credit rating of AA cannot exceed 20 percent.

- *The maximum allocation for any individual credit:* With the exception of bonds that have the full faith and credit backing of the U.S. government, or are the bonds of U.S. government agencies or GSEs, no single issuer can exceed the following: AAA-rated bonds 20 percent, AA-rated bonds 10 percent, and A-rated bonds 5 percent.

- *The types of instruments that are excluded from eligibility:* Neither MBS nor hybrid securities can be purchased.

- *The minimum and maximum block size:* Individual bonds should not be purchased in amounts less than $50,000 nor greater than $250,000. A maximum is recommended to ensure sufficient diversification of credit risk. A minimum is recommended because if there were an opportunity to harvest a loss a small block would lead to high trading costs.

It is critical that investors understand that even having a well-thought-out plan, and a signed investment policy statement, is only a *necessary* condition for being a successful investor. The *sufficient* condition is having the discipline to stay the course and ignore the noise of the market and the emotions it causes, such as greed and envy, and fear and panic, so that you adhere to your well-thought-out plan. The IPS should be reviewed on a regular basis. One reason for doing so is to remind yourself why you adopted the specific strategy. A second reason is that an IPS should be a living document. Personal circumstances can alter one's ability, willingness, and need to take risk.

CHAPTER TWELVE

◆

Summary

As I traipse around the country speaking to investing groups, or just stay in my cage writing my articles, I'm often accused of "disempowering" people because I refuse to give any credence to anyone's hope of beating the market. The knowledge that I don't need to know anything is an incredibly profound form of knowledge. Personally, I think it's the ultimate form of empowerment. You can't tune out the massive industry of investment prediction unless you want to: otherwise, you'll never have the fortitude to stop listening. But if you can plug your ears to every attempt (by anyone) to predict what the markets will do, you will outperform nearly every other investor alive over the long run. Only the mantra of "I don't know, and I don't care" will get you there. —Jason Zweig, series writer for *Money* magazine

If you want to see the greatest threat to your financial future, go home and take a look in the mirror.
—Jonathan Clements, financial columnist
for the *Wall Street Journal*

We have completed our journey through the world of fixed-income investing. Now that you are an informed investor you should be able to avoid being exploited by those who might take advantage of the lack of knowledge the general public has about fixed-income investing. You should also be able to avoid many of the mistakes individual investors make. Informed investors generally make far better investment decisions.

Summary

Hopefully, you now recognize that while the world of fixed-income investing is filled with complexity, the winning strategy is actually quite simple. To summarize, the winning strategy is to:

- Write and sign an IPS that defines your objective, risk tolerance, investment strategy, and eligible securities (i.e., maximum maturity and minimum credit rating).

- Purchase assets from the highest investment grades, generally avoiding instruments with a rating below AA.

- Avoid securities with complex features, as they are products generally meant to be sold (by brokers), not bought (by investors).

- Avoid trying to outperform the market either by trying to guess the direction of interest rates or by trying to identify securities that have been somehow mispriced by the market. There is simply no credible evidence that investors, either individuals or institutions, are *likely* to succeed in this effort. As Peter Bernstein points out: "The essence of investment theory is that being smart is not a sufficient condition for being rich."[1] The winning strategy is to be a buy-and-hold investor.

- Purchase assets with maturities that are short to intermediate in term, avoiding long-term bonds. If the main objective of the fixed-income allocation is to reduce overall portfolio risk, then maturities should be restricted to the short end of the curve (maximum of two to three years). If the goal is to generate greater cash flow or to manage reinvestment risk, then maturities can be stretched to the intermediate part of the curve (five to ten years, depending on the location of the "sweet spot").

- Avoid the purchase of hybrid securities.

- If using mutual funds (or ETFs) to gain access to the fixed-income market, invest in only very low cost, passively managed vehicles. The same advice applies to selecting separate account managers. Avoid mutual funds that have loads.

- If building your own portfolio of individual bonds, restrict purchases to the primary (new issue) market. This is especially true of municipal and corporate bonds. If, however, you have access to the secondary market through a fee-only advisor or separate account manager who can buy at or near wholesale prices, the secondary market may provide more attractive alternatives.

- Since the prudent strategy is to be a buy-and-hold-to-maturity investor, it is not necessary to "pay up" for liquidity (all else being equal, the more liquid the asset, the lower the yield). Thus investors who plan on holding to maturity should at least consider buying less-liquid securities (e.g., issues from smaller municipalities that do not frequently come to market) for some portion of the portfolio—as long as the credit rating is AAA or AA. Less-liquid securities should not, however, constitute the bulk of your portfolio. The reasons are that there may be unanticipated calls on your capital and there may be opportunities to harvest tax losses. Selling less-liquid securities is likely to result in having to accept large markdowns.

- Review your IPS on an annual basis as well as whenever the assumptions you made about your ability, willingness, and need to take risk have changed.

Hopefully, you have enjoyed the journey through the world of fixed-income investing. It is now time for you to write, and sign, your IPS. As you go through that process we urge you to carefully consider these words of wisdom: "The inconvenience of going from rich to poor is greater than most people can tolerate. Staying rich requires an entirely different approach from getting rich. It might be said that one *gets* rich by working hard and taking big risks, and that one *stays* rich by limiting risk and not spending too much."[2]

In closing, we offer these words of caution from legendary investor Pogo: "We have met the enemy and he is us." Do not take more risk than you have the ability, willingness, or need to take.

AFTERWORD

◆

Some Light Is Finally Being Shed on Municipal Bond Prices

In 1990 a computerized pricing system called GovPX was introduced. The system had a major impact on the market for Treasury securities as real-time pricing information became available to investors. The increase in transparency of pricing led to a reduction of trading costs—bid-offer spreads narrowed. Finally, in 2005, technology that had existed for fifteen years became available to municipal bond investors.

On January 31, 2005, the Municipal Securities Rulemaking Board (MSRB), through its Transaction Reporting Program (TRP), began making real-time pricing information for all municipal bond trades available within fifteen minutes of a trade. Previously, such information had been disseminated the day after the trade. More importantly, at least as far as retail investors are concerned, the new MSRB data is posted free of charge on the Bond Market Association's Web site, www.InvestinginBonds.com. The Web site allows investors to view municipal transactions by state, maturity, insurance coverage, credit rating, and call date. Investors are also able to view the security's daily high and low, along with its trading history.

This initiative has two objectives. The first is to ensure that retail investors have the information they need to make investment decisions. The second objective is to provide an audit trail of transactions that can be used for market surveillance and the enforcement of MSRB rules by regulatory bodies such as the SEC and the MSRB.

In an effort similar to the MSRBs, on February 7, 2005, the National Association of Securities Dealers (NASD) began the dissemination of price and transaction data on 99 percent of the universe of corporate bonds—approximately twenty-nine thousand of them. The remaining 1 percent are special issues subject to delayed reporting and are almost exclusively the domain of institutional investors.

Impact on Investors

While information has become more quickly disseminated in the municipal bond market, unfortunately, the impact is likely to be negligible. The reason is that the structure of the municipal bond market is radically different from the structure of the Treasury, corporate bond, and equity markets.

As we have discussed, the U.S. Treasury market is comprised of a single issuer and relatively few outstanding debt securities. The corporate bond market contains about thirty thousand issues. The equity market contains about seven to eight thousand individual issues. In comparison to these three markets, the municipal bond market contains approximately 1.7 million individual issues from approximately fifty thousand different issuers.

As we noted in chapter 3, less than 30 percent of municipal bonds will trade in any given year. In addition, less than 1 percent of municipal bonds trade on a daily basis, and only 10 percent of bonds that do trade on a given day trade as often as four times that day—and there is only a one in three chance of repeating that on the following day.[1] With such a small percentage of the outstanding securities being traded on a regular basis, it is hard to imagine how the dissemination of pricing information can impact the bid-offer spreads to which the retail market will be subject.

Another reason we are pessimistic about the impact on retail trading costs is that while the reporting of municipal bond trades is now centralized by a computerized repository, the actual trading in the secondary market for municipal bonds remains *decentralized*. Because the municipal bond market is decentralized, there is not a single clearinghouse for the trading of all municipal securities. The lack of a centralized system prevents participants from comparing all the bids and offers and thus trading on the tightest spreads. The result is that market makers (broker-dealers) provide their own bids and offers to retail investors without the competitive pressures that a centralized exchange would present. A retail investor looking to buy or sell a particular security must first locate a market participant, get the bid or offer on that security, and then call another market maker to compare quotes. If the security in question is not in the second dealer's inventory, or if the second dealer is not particularly eager to own the security in his inventory (in the case of a customer sale), there is the distinct possibility that the dealer will not even make a bid or offer for the customer to compare to the first dealer's quote—and the process would have to continue. Clearly, this is not an efficient process for retail investors. In addition, as long as the broker-dealer is the entity setting prices, prices will almost certainly be set to the customer's disadvantage.

Appendix A

Callable Bonds: Risk and Return

As we have discussed, callable bonds are securities that give the issuer the right, but not the obligation, to call the bond (prepay) prior to maturity. The issuer will exercise this right if they are able to reissue the debt at lower interest rates, once all costs of a recall and new issuance are taken into consideration. The issuer will also exercise the right to call if their credit rating has improved enough to allow them to replace the existing debt with a lower-cost security. The issuer pays a premium to the purchaser of the note in return for the purchaser's accepting the risk of prepayment (and then having to reinvest the proceeds at a lower rate). The size of the premium will depend on several factors, including the term of the call rights (when does the right to call the bond begin and end) and the price at which the borrower must repurchase the bond (sometimes it is above par). The question for the investor considering purchasing callable bonds is: Is the incremental return worth the reinvestment risk? As with most investment issues there is no one right answer, just one right answer for each investor (and even then *only* before the fact).

When an investor purchases a bond with a call feature, the

investor receives an incremental yield. In return for the benefit of the higher yield, the investor is now at risk should interest rates fall significantly, as the bond could be called by the issuer.

When analyzing whether a callable bond is an appropriate investment, the investor should consider whether the higher yield is sufficient compensation for the risk that falling rates or other reasons will lead to early redemption of the bond. The answer will depend on whether the investor is more damaged by rising or falling interest rates. If the greater risk to the investor were rising interest rates, buying a callable bond would seem prudent. In a rising-rate environment the investor will not only receive a higher interest rate (the call premium), but the higher rate also makes the bond more defensive (because it has a somewhat shorter duration)—it will not fall in value as much. If the greater risk to the investor were falling interest rates, buying a callable bond would be imprudent.

Consider the following: If an investor could meet her cash flow needs at current interest rate levels without taking call risk, but could not do so at a lower interest rate, accepting call risk may be imprudent. On the other hand, if she could still meet cash flow needs at lower rate levels, it might be prudent to consider taking the risk in return for the greater potential reward, as well as some incremental protection against rising rates.

There is another issue to consider. If the investor holds a mortgage, or any other debt, this liability should be considered in the decision-making process (debt of any type should be treated as a negative position in fixed-income assets for asset allocation purposes). The risk of callable bonds shows up when rates fall. If an investor also holds a fixed-rate mortgage, she might benefit from falling rates by refinancing at the lower current rate (or if the mortgage is an adjustable-rate mortgage the rate would automatically move lower). The benefit from refinancing the mortgage would offset the "loss" of future returns experienced from the bond being called. The size of the offset would depend on the size of the bond holding relative to the size of the mortgage. If the investor in a callable bond (who earns the call premium by selling the call to the issuer) also holds a mortgage at (or above) current interest rates she would, in effect, be recovering the call premium she paid the mortgage lender for the right to prepay should rates fall. Of course this depends on the rate on the mortgage relative to current market rates. If the mortgage rate is well below market, there may not be an opportunity to refinance should rates fall. It may also depend on changes in the shape of the yield curve. For example, if she has a mortgage that adjusts to a short-term rate and only longer rates fall, there will be no benefit, but her bond will be called. Thus each circumstance is unique and should be carefully considered.

Callable bonds are worth considering, but they are not right for every investor.

Appendix B

Real Return versus Nominal Return Fixed-Income Assets: An Investment Strategy

The guarantee of a real return is what differentiates TIPS (and I bonds) from other fixed-income investments, the coupon rate of which is not adjusted for inflation. Thus TIPS provide a guaranteed *real* return to maturity while other fixed-income investments provide a guaranteed *nominal* rate of return. The question for the investor then is: How do I decide how much, if any, to allocate to TIPS versus nominal return bonds.

The Benefits of TIPS

As we have discussed, the hedge against inflation risk makes TIPS an attractive investment alternative, particularly for those at the greatest risk from rising inflation. There is, however, another benefit of TIPS that should not be overlooked. All fixed-income assets of high credit quality have low correlation with risky equities. The longer the maturity of a fixed-income asset, however, the higher the correlation of its returns to the returns on equities.

Because equities actually have a slightly negative short-term correlation with inflation (inflation has a negative impact on equity returns as it increases business risk), TIPS should logically have a negative correlation with equities (as they are positively correlated with inflation)—and they have during their relatively brief history. This negative correlation helps reduce the overall risk of the portfolio. This is a distinct advantage over intermediate to longer-term bonds that have positive (though still low) correlation with equities. Therefore, given that investors are on average risk averse, it is logical to believe that they are willing to accept a slightly lower expected return on TIPS than on a nominal coupon bond of similar maturity. A third benefit of TIPS is that they have lower expected volatility than conventional Treasury bonds because *nominal* interest rates are more volatile than *real* rates.

Lower Risk and Lower Expected Return

Let's look at how the market might price the real return on TIPS. Let's assume that a ten-year Treasury bond yielded 4 percent and that the market expected inflation of 2 percent. Thus the expected real return on this instrument would be 2 percent. Given the aforementioned risk aversion of investors, TIPS might be expected to yield say 1.75 percent. The 0.25 percent lower expected return can be thought of as the risk premium investors are willing to pay to guarantee a real return. (Note that there is no way to measure how much of the difference between the 4 percent yield on the ten-year Treasury and the TIPS is explained by the expected inflation rate and how much is explained by the insurance premium.) If inflation turns out to be more (less) than 2.25 percent (4 minus 1.75), then TIPS will have provided higher (lower) returns.

Given that TIPS have a lower expected return than similar-maturity nominal-return coupon bonds, a question for investors is how to decide if the insurance premium is worth the price paid to hedge the risk of inflation. This is particularly important since similar protection against the risk of inflation can be obtained by purchasing short-term (instead of long-term) fixed-income investments. A short maturity results in yields adjusting upward due to rising inflation with only a short lag—and the shorter the maturity, the less the inflation risk. Thus both TIPS and short-term nominal-return investments provide a hedge against inflation. And note that while TIPS have a slightly negative correlation with equities, short-term fixed-income instruments (up to about one year) have virtually no correlation with equities, and longer-term bonds have positive correlation (the longer, the higher the correlation). Note also that there is another significant difference between TIPS and short-term fixed-income instruments—TIPS have more price risk—they are much more volatile—because they are exposed to changes in real interest rates.

Now let's consider an investor who has a high aversion to the risks of inflation. Thus he does not want to consider longer-term bonds. He may also not be comfortable with the higher correlation with equities of longer-term bonds. Thus this investor is trying to decide if he should purchase either a TIPS or, say, a one-year Treasury instrument. One major difference between the two from a risk perspective is that TIPS provide a guaranteed real return (until maturity) while the one-year Treasury instrument will provide a floating real rate of return. Since there is no evidence that investors can forecast which strategy will provide the higher return over the full period, perhaps a good strategy is to hedge the risk of changing real rates of return—purchasing some TIPS and some one-year instruments. However, investors for whom the consequences of a fall in real rates are negative might prefer TIPS. Those for whom the negative consequences of a rise in real rates are greater might prefer the one-year Treasury. However, there might be another consideration—the current yield on TIPS. Note that as of this writing (January 2005) the Treasury currently issues only ten-year TIPS (which we will use in our examples). However the Treasury had also recently announced that they would begin offering twenty-year TIPS (and they previously had issued thirty-year TIPS, though the issuance of that maturity was ended in 2002).

We begin by examining the historical real return on longer-term bonds. For the period 1926–2004 longer-term Treasury bonds have provided a real return of 2.4 percent. While we cannot know exactly how much of a risk premium the market is willing to pay in order to hedge the inflation risk inherent in longer-term bonds, we might guess that it might be something on the order of 0.25 percent. And the price investors are willing to pay will logically depend on the volatility of inflation. Thus investors in Brazil, with a long history of periods of extremely high inflation, would likely be willing to pay a steeper premium than would U.S. or Swiss investors. Even in the United States, however, we would not expect this premium to remain constant. Of course each investor can determine for herself how much she might be willing to pay based on her unique situation and tolerance for risk. We need a little more information before we can develop a strategy.

Logically, there should be some relationship between the real growth of the economy and the real rate on bonds. With this assumption we can develop a disciplined strategy to determine how much an investor should allocate to TIPS and how much to nominal-return bonds. The long-term real growth rate of the U.S. economy has been about 3 percent. Thus we might expect that the real return on bonds should not be much above that. And, as we have seen, it has actually been somewhat below that. Of course, there is a natural limit of zero (almost certainly it is higher than that) to how low the real rate could fall. So perhaps we might consider that in most cases the real yield on TIPS might be expected to range between 1 and 4 percent. Since TIPS prices move in inverse relationship to their real yield, when real yields are at the lower end of the range the price risk on TIPS is probably much greater than when yields are at the higher end of the range. Also buying at the higher end of the range allows the investor to "lock in" the high yield while buying at the low end may result in investors "locking in" a low real return.

Developing a Strategy

We are now ready to develop a strategy that will help you decide on an allocation between TIPS and nominal-return fixed-income instruments. Before providing a specific formula, however, note that there is no "right" answer here. The "right" answer will be determined by each investor's own willingness and ability to take the risk of unexpected inflation negatively impacting his portfolio and

**Decision Table for Allocation Between Short-Term
Fixed-Income and Ten-Year TIPS**

Real Yield on TIPS	Allocation to TIPS
> 3%	75–100%
> 2.5% < 3%	50–75%
> 2% < 2.5%	25–50%
> 1.5% < 2%	0–25%
< 1.5%	0%

> = greater than, < = less than

lifestyle. However, it is important to develop a disciplined strategy so that an investor is not reacting to the noise of the market and the emotions that noise can cause. With that in mind the table above is offered as a suggested strategy (one which you should tailor to your specific situation) to determine the percent allocation to TIPS versus nominal-return bonds.

Ranges have been provided because each investor has different risk concerns. For example, those more concerned about the risk of inflation might consider the higher end of the suggested allocation to be more appropriate. In addition, they might even be willing to lower the required yields in the left-hand column.

Implementation

The table should be used in the following manner. If the real yield on ten-year TIPS were 2.6 percent, then an investor would allocate between 50 and 75 percent of their fixed-income assets to TIPS and 25 to 50 percent to nominal-return instruments (a specific number should be chosen up front and made part of the investment policy statement). It is critical, however, to consider trading costs. In order to prevent unnecessary trading costs caused by movements slightly above and then below the targets, the targeted rates should be treated as buy ranges—they should be used to make purchase decisions for new investments. A hold range of perhaps 0.25 percent should be created for sell purposes. For example, let's assume that the real rate on TIPS fell from 2.6 percent to 2.4 percent. What should our investor do with his current portfolio? Nothing—unless the rate fell to 2.25 percent (2.5 minus 0.25). If new cash was available for investment, however, the new cash could be used to move the allocation toward or even to

50 percent (the targeted allocation when the real rate is 2.4 percent. Note that even if there are no trading costs (as might be the case with mutual funds) we would not want to be having to alter positions with every small move in rates above and then below the targeted levels. Note that this type of strategy creates a buy low and sell high environment. When the real rate on TIPS is high, investors are buying when TIPS prices are low. And they are selling TIPS when the real rate is low and prices are high.

Note that the use of the above table does not imply that when the real yield is low (high) that TIPS are overvalued (undervalued). The market is highly efficient, meaning that the current price (yield) is the best estimate of the correct price. Thus the table is not meant to convey that by using it an investor will receive above-market returns by exploiting mispricing, and thus outperform a buy-and-hold investor. The table is provided as a risk management tool only. The underlying philosophy is that because of a natural limited expected range for the yield on TIPS, when yields are low, the price risk is greater on the downside then the upside, and vice versa. That says nothing about the likelihood of an event occurring. To clarify, if the real yield on TIPS is currently 1.5 percent (near the lower end of the expected range), that tells us nothing about the likelihood of its rising or falling from that level. However, if the assumption is correct about the expected range for TIPS yields, if the yield fell, it is not likely to fall much (prices will not rise much). On the other hand, if rates rise, they could rise a great deal, and prices could fall dramatically. The reverse situation would be true if current yields were high.

TIPS versus Long-Term Bonds

The same kind of analysis can be applied to the decision whether to purchase long-term bonds or TIPS. There are many investors for whom the main role of fixed-income investing is maintaining a stable cash flow (as opposed to minimizing portfolio risk). By extending maturity they can be assured of a known *nominal* return over a longer time frame (reducing the risk that falling interest rates can have on one's lifestyle). In addition, if the yield curve is positively sloped, incremental yield can be gained. These benefits, however, come with increased risks in other areas. As noted, the correlation with equities will increase as the maturity extends. In addition, price risk and exposure to unexpected inflation is increased. So careful consideration must be given to weighing the risks and rewards of extending maturities. For those investors willing to accept the risks of longer maturities, they, too, have choices. They can build a portfolio of individual securities, own a longer-term bond fund, or they can purchase longer-term TIPS (currently TIPS can be bought with a maturity as far out as 2032, and while the Treasury has canceled sales of thirty-year TIPS, they have announced the sale of twenty-year TIPS).

Decision Table for Allocation Between Long-Term Fixed-Income and Ten-Year TIPS

Real Yield on TIPS	Allocation to TIPS
> 3.25%	75–100%
> 2.75% < 3.25%	50–75%
> 2.25% < 2.75%	25–50%
> 1.75% < 2.25%	0–25%
< 1.75%	0%

> = greater than, < = less than

The investor in longer-term securities can also generate a table that should be part of the IPS that provides them discipline in allocating between TIPS and longer-term bonds. Given that the real return on long-term bonds should be higher than on short-term bonds, the required yields in the left-hand column of the table might be increased by twenty-five basis points, resulting in a table that looks like the one above.

Notes

Chapter One: Bondspeak

1. Brian Reynolds, "Pulling the Trigger on Bonds," www.thestreet.com/_tscs/comment/numbersgame/1248468.html, January 10, 2001.
2. William J. Bernstein, *The Four Pillars of Investing* (McGraw-Hill, 2002), p. 297.

Chapter Two: The Risks of Fixed-Income Investing

1. Benoit B. Mandelbrot and Richard L. Hudson, *The (Mis)Behavior of Markets* (Basic Books, 2004), p. 24.
2. UBS Paine-Webber Inc., "Impact of the President's Tax Reform Plan Upon the Municipal Market," Research Update, January 17, 2003.
3. A.G. Edwards, "Municipal Industrial Development Bonds," Research Report, April 12, 2005.
4. Pavan Wadhwa, "Municipals as an Asset Class," *Journal of Investing* (Summer 2005).
5. A.G. Edwards.
6. Fitch, "Municipal Default Risk Revisited," fitchratings.com, June 23, 2003.

Chapter Three: The Buying and Selling of Individual Bonds

1. Lynn Hume, "Judge Dismisses SEC Case Against Former Broker, Rules Markups Not Excessive," *Bond Buyer,* May 1, 2002.

Chapter Four: How the Fixed-Income Markets Really Work

1. Michael C. Jensen, "Some Anomalous Evidence Regarding Market Efficiency," *Journal of Financial Economics* (June/September 1978).
2. Mark M. Carhart, "On Persistence in Mutual Fund Performance," *Journal of Finance* (March 1997).
3. American Law Institute Third Restatement of the Law, Chapter 7 (The Administration of the Trust), Topic 5 (Investment of Trust Funds), Section 227, "General Note on Comments e through h," subtitle Market Efficiency.
4. W. Scott Simon, *The Prudent Investor Act,* p. vii.
5. Christopher R. Blake, Edwin J. Elton, and Martin J. Gruber, "The Performance of Bond Mutual Funds," *Journal of Business* (July 1993).
6. Kevin Stephenson, "Just How Bad Are Economists at Predicting Interest Rates?" *Journal of Investing* (Summer 1997).
7. John Bogle, *Bogle on Mutual Funds* (Irwin, 1994), pp. 113–114.
8. Russel Kinnel, "Time to Clear Out the Dead Wood," Morningstar FundInvestor, December 2004, p. 3.
9. William Sherden, *The Fortune Sellers* (Wiley, 1998), pp. 61–67.
10. David Altany, "New Jobs for the Number Crunchers," *Industry Week,* April 20, 1992, p. 76.
11. Michael Lewis, *Moneyball* (Norton, 2003), p. 66.
12. Dimensional Fund Advisors.
13. Ibid.
14. Antti Ilmanen, Rory Byrne, Heinz Gunasekera, and Robert Minikin, "Which Risks Have Been Best Rewarded?" *Journal of Portfolio Management,* Winter 2004.

Chapter Five: The Securities of the U.S. Treasury, Government Agencies, and Government-Sponsored Enterprises

1. www.geology.sdsu.edu/classes/geol351/03floods/floodslect.htm.

Chapter Seven: The World of Corporate Fixed-Income Securities

1. Edwin J. Elton, Martin J. Gruber, Deepak Agrawal, and Christopher Mann, "Explaining the Rate Spread on Corporate Bonds," *Journal of Finance* (February 2001).

2. Ulf Herold and Raimond Maurer, "How Much Credit?" *Journal of Fixed Income* (March 2003).

3. Laurence Gonzales, *Deep Survival* (Norton, 2003), p. 134.

Chapter Eight: The World of International Fixed-Income Securities

1. Truman A. Clark, "Does Foreign-Exchange Hedging Reduce Risk in Global Portfolios?" February 2000 (www.dfaus.com).

2. Annette Thau, The Bond Book, 2d. ed. (McGraw-Hill, 1992), p. 226.

3. Claude B. Erb, Campbell R. Harvey, and Tadas E. Viskanta, "Understanding Emerging Markets Bonds," *Emerging Markets Quarterly* (Spring 2000).

4. Ibid.

5. Ibid.

Chapter Ten: The World of Municipal Bonds

1. "Municipal Rating Transitions and Defaults," Standard and Poor's, June 13, 2001.

2. Advertised yield for Schwab Value Advantage Money Fund–Investor Shares. https://ssl.schwabinstitutional.com, July 2, 2004.

3 Coupon rate for Missouri State Health & Educational municipal bond (VAR–Washington University–SER C), Bloomberg, July 2, 2004.

Chapter Eleven: How to Design and Construct Your Fixed-Income Portfolio

1. Robert M. Damnion, Chester S. Spatt, and Harold H. Zhang, "Optimal Asset Location and Allocation with Taxable and Tax-Deferred Investing," *Journal of Finance* (June 2004).

2. Ibid.

3. Ibid.

Chapter Twelve: Summary

1. Peter L. Bernstein, *The Portable MBA in Investment* (Wiley, 1995), p. 1.

2. *Investment Management*, edited by Peter L. Bernstein and Aswath Damodaran (Wiley, 1998), p. 379.

Afterword

1. *Report on Transactions in Municipal Securities*, Office of Economic Analysis and Office of Municipal Securities, Securities and Exchange Commission.

Glossary

401(k) A defined contribution plan offered by a corporation to its employees, that allows employees to set aside tax-deferred income for retirement purposes.

403(b) A retirement plan offered by nonprofit organizations, such as universities and charitable organizations, rather than corporations. Similar to a 401(k) plan.

Accrued interest Interest accumulated on a bond or note since the last interest payment or from the effective date of a new issue as determined by its underwriters (often the same day as the issue date). Since interest on municipal bonds is payable semiannually, when you buy a bond in midterm you are only entitled to the interest the bond earns after you buy it. The interest earned previously, the accrued interest, belongs to the seller.

Active management The attempt to uncover securities the market has either undervalued or overvalued; also the attempt to time investment decisions in order to be more heavily invested when the market is rising and less so when the market is falling.

Agency risk A risk that only applies to investors in funds, or separate accounts. There is always some risk that the manager will act in his or her own best interest and not in the best interest of investors. There is also the risk of fraud.

Alternative minimum tax (AMT) A method of calculating federal income tax. Interest on some private activity municipal bonds is subject to the AMT if the bondholder calculates the federal income tax using the AMT.

Asset allocation The process of determining what percentage of assets should be dedicated to which specific asset classes. Also the outcome of that process.

Asset class A group of assets with similar risk and reward characteristics. Cash, debt instruments, real estate, and equities are examples of asset classes. Within a general asset class, such as equities, there are more specific classes such as large-cap stocks and small-cap stocks, and domestic and international stocks.

Average life The length of time that will pass before one half of a debt obligation has been retired. Usually refers to mortgage-backed securities.

Basis point One one-hundredth of one percent (1/100 % or 0.01 percent). Thus 25 basis points equal one-quarter of one percent, 100 basis points equal one percent.

Bid An offer to buy at a specified price or yield. Also, the price at which a dealer is willing to buy a security.

Bid-offer spread See SPREAD.

Bond A negotiable instrument (distinguishing it from a loan) evidencing a legal agreement to compensate the lender through periodic interest payments and the repayment of principal in full on a stipulated date.

Bond premium The amount by which a bond or note is bought or sold above its par value (or face value) without considering accrued interest, if any.

Broker-dealer Any individual or firm in the business of buying and selling securities for itself and others. Broker-dealers must register with the SEC. When acting as a broker, a broker-dealer executes orders on behalf of his or her client. When acting as a dealer, a broker-dealer executes trades for his or her firm's own account. Securities bought for the firm's own account may be sold to clients or other firms, or become a part of the firm's holdings.

Callable bond A bond or note that is subject to redemption at the option of the issuer prior to its stated maturity. The call date and call premium, if any, are stated in the offering statement or broker's confirmation.

Call premium The percentage above the principal amount of a bond that is paid by the issuer when they call the bond.

Collateralized mortgage obligation (CMO) A mortgage-backed bond that separates pools of fixed-rate mortgages into different expected maturity classes. The collateral for a CMO can be either residential or commercial mortgages.

Commercial paper Short-term, unsecured promissory notes issued primarily by corporations.

Convertible Security that can be exchanged for a specified amount of another, related security, at the option of the issuer or the holder.

Convexity The rate of change of duration as yields change. See NEGATIVE CONVEXITY and POSITIVE CONVEXITY.

Correlation In statistics, correlation is the measure of the strength of the linear relationship between two variables. Values can range from +1.00 (perfect correlation) to −1.00 (perfect negative correlation).

Coupon rate The specified annual interest rate payable to the bond or note holder as printed on the bond.

Coverage The margin of safety for payment of debt service on a bond that reflects the number of times the actual or estimated earnings (or revenue if a revenue bond) for a one-year period exceeds debt service that is payable.

Currency risk The risk that an investment's value will be affected by changes in exchange rates.

Current interest bond A bond that pays interest at regular intervals, as opposed to a zero-coupon bond.

Current yield The ratio of the coupon rate on a bond to the current price expressed as a percentage. Thus if you pay par, or 100 cents on the dollar, for your bond and the coupon rate is 6 percent, the current yield is 6 percent; however, if you pay 97 for your 6 percent discount bond the current yield is 6.186 percent (0.06 divided by 97). If you pay 102 for a 6 percent bond the current yield is 5.88 percent (0.06 divided by 102).

CUSIP number A unique number assigned to publicly traded individual securities by the Committee on Uniform Security Identification Procedures.

Debenture An unsecured bond that is backed by the issuer's legally binding promise to pay.

De minimis rule As it pertains to individual holders of municipal bonds, the de minimis rule allows a small amount of market discount on a bond to be taxed at the capital-gains tax rate. Under the de minimis rule, up to a maximum of one-quarter of a point of discount per full year between purchase date and the maturity or sale date is taxed at the capital gains tax rate. However, once the market discount exceeds that amount, all of the market discount becomes taxable at the ordinary income tax rate.

Default Failure to pay in a timely manner principal or interest. See also TECHNICAL DEFAULT.

Denomination The face amount of a security.

Discount The percent by which the market value of a bond is less than par value or face value.

Discount bond A bond selling at a dollar price below par and whose yield therefore exceeds the coupon rate.

Duration The percentage change in the price of a bond that can be expected given a percentage change in the yield on that bond. A higher duration number indicates a greater sensitivity of that bond's price to changes in interest rates.

EAFE Index The Europe, Australasia, and Far East Index is similar to the S&P 500 Index in that it consists of the stocks of the large companies from the EAFE countries. The stocks within the index are weighted by market capitalization.

Efficient Frontier Model A model based on the assumption that investors care about the volatility of their portfolio, in addition to its expected return. The model computes portfolios (mixes of risky investments) that have the highest expected return for every attainable level of volatility.

Efficient market A state in which investors can't use trading systems to increase their expected return without at the same time increasing the risks to which they are exposed.

Efficient markets hypothesis (EMH) A hypothesis explaining how markets work. See EFFICIENT MARKET.

Emerging markets The capital markets of less-developed countries that are beginning to develop characteristics of developed countries, such as higher per capita income. Countries typically included in this category would be Brazil, Mexico, and Thailand.

Exchange-traded fund (ETF) For practical purposes these act like open-ended, no-load mutual funds. Like mutual funds, they can be created to represent virtually any index or asset class. ETFs represent a cross between an exchange-listed stock and an open-ended, no-load mutual fund. Like stocks (but unlike mutual funds), they trade throughout the day.

Event risk The risk that something unexpected will occur (e.g., war, political crisis, flood, hurricane) that will negatively impact the value of a security.

Face value For a debt security, the amount paid to the investor at maturity.

Forward currency contract An agreement to buy or sell a country's currency at a specific price, usually thirty, sixty, or ninety days in the future. This guarantees an exchange rate on a given date. It is typically used to hedge risk (i.e. currency risk).

Full faith and credit The pledge that all taxing powers and resources, without limitation, will, if necessary, be used to repay a debt obligation.

Fundamental security analysis The attempt to discover mispriced securities by focusing on predicting future earnings.

Futures contract An agreement to purchase or sell a specific collection of securities or a physical commodity at a specified price and time in the future. For example, an S&P 500 futures contract represents ownership interest in the S&P 500 Index at a specified price for delivery on a specific date on a particular exchange.

General obligation bond (GO) A bond secured by a pledge of the issuer's tax revenue. For example, the general obligation bonds of local governments are paid from property taxes and other general revenues. See REVENUE BOND.

Government-sponsored enterprises (GSE) Privately held corporations with public purposes created by the U.S. Congress to reduce the cost of capital for certain borrowing sectors of the economy. GSEs carry the implicit moral backing of the U.S. government, but they are not direct obligations of the U.S. government.

High-yield bond See JUNK BOND.

Hybrid security A security that has both equity and fixed-income characteristics. Examples of hybrids are convertible bonds, preferred stocks, and junk bonds.

I bond A U.S. government bond that provides both a fixed rate of return and an inflation-protection component. The principal value of the bond increases by the total of the fixed rate and the inflation component. The income is deferred for federal tax purposes until funds are withdrawn from the account holding the bond and is exempt from state and local income tax.

Indenture A legal document describing in specific detail the terms and conditions of a bond offering, the rights of the bondholder, and the obligations of the issuer to the bondholder. It identifies the issuer and their obligations, conditions of default, and actions that holders may take in the event of a default. It also identifies such issues as call features, sinking fund requirements, and the day-count method upon which accrued interest is calculated.

Index fund A passively managed fund that seeks to replicate the performance of a particular index by buying all, or a representative sample, of the securities in that index in direct proportion to their weight by market capitalization within that index and holding them.

Industrial development bond (IDB) A bond used to finance facilities for private enterprises, water and air pollution control, ports, airports, resource-recovery plants, housing, and so on. The bonds are backed by the credit of the private corporation borrower rather than by the credit of the issuer. Also known as conduit bonds and industrial revenue bonds (IRBs).

Interest-only bond See IO STRIP.

Inverse floater A security whose interest rate varies with a short-term interest rate index in such a way that the yield is inversely related to the market rate of interest.

Investment grade A bond whose credit qualities are at least adequate to maintain debt service, but which may also have some speculative qualities. Moody's Investors Service investment grade ratings are Baa and higher. Standard & Poor's are BBB and higher. Below investment grade ratings suggest a primarily speculative credit quality.

IO strip A security based solely on interest payments from a bond (e.g., a mortgage-backed bond). After the principal has been repaid, interest payments stop, and the value of the IO falls to nothing.

IPS Investment policy statement.

IRA A tax-deferred individual retirement account.

Junk bond A bond rated below investment grade. Also referred to as a high-yield bond.

Kurtosis The degree to which exceptional values, much larger or smaller than the average, occur more frequently (high kurtosis) or less frequently (low kurtosis) than in a normal (bell shaped) distribution. High kurtosis results in exceptional values that are called "fat tails." Low kurtosis results in "thin tails."

Liquidity A measure of the ease of trading a security in the market.

Markdown The amount by which the price received by a retail investor selling a bond is *less than* the wholesale price (the price in the interdealer market).

MARS Municipal Auction Rate Securities (see chapter 10).

Markup The amount by which the price paid for a bond by a retail investor is *greater than* the wholesale price (the price in the interdealer market).

Maturity The date upon which the issuer promises to repay the principal.

Mean variance analysis Evaluation of risky investment alternatives based on the expected return and variance of all possible portfolios. The goal is to identify portfolios with the highest possible expected return for every level of risk (or, equivalently, the least risky portfolios for every level of expected return). In mean variance analysis, risk is defined as the volatility of a portfolio, measured by the variance of returns.

Mortgage-backed security (MBS) A financial instrument representing an interest in assets that are mortgage related (either commercial or residential).

MSRB The Municipal Securities Rulemaking Board. The self-regulatory body with jurisdiction over municipal bond dealers. The Securities and Exchange Commission must approve any rules proposed by the MSRB.

Municipal bond A bond issued by any of the fifty states, U.S. territories, and their subdivisions, counties, cities, towns, villages, and school districts, agencies, such as authorities and special districts created by the states, and certain federally sponsored agencies such as local housing authorities. Interest paid on theses bonds is generally exempt from federal income taxes and is also generally exempt from state and local taxes in the state of issuance.

Municipal notes Short-term municipal obligations, generally maturing in one year or less. The most common types are bond anticipation notes (BANs), revenue anticipation notes (RANs), tax anticipation notes (TANs), grant anticipation notes, project notes, and construction loan notes.

NAV Net asset value. For a mutual fund, the NAV is the total value of portfolio holdings minus the total value of all liabilities. The NAV is usually calculated on a daily basis, and is quoted per share (e.g. NAV is $14.68 per share).

Negative convexity If its duration decreases when interest rates fall, a security exhibits negative convexity.

Nominal returns Returns that have not been adjusted for the impact of inflation.

Offer The price or yield at which a security is offered for sale.

Original issue discount (OID) Some maturities of a new bond issue have an offering price below par. The appreciation from the original price to par over the life of the bonds is treated as tax-exempt income and is not subject to capital-gains tax.

Par Most bonds have a face value of $1,000. They are also traded in blocks of a minimum of $1,000. Par, or 100 percent, is considered $1,000.

Passive management A buy-and-hold investment strategy, specifically contrary to active management. Characteristics of the passive-management approach include lower portfolio turnover, lower operating expenses and transactions costs, greater tax efficiency, fully invested at all times, no style drift, and a long-term perspective.

PO strip A security based solely on principal payments from a bond (e.g., a mortgage-backed bond).

Positive convexity If its duration increases when interest rates fall, a security exhibits positive convexity.

Premium The amount, if any, by which the price exceeds the principal amount (par value) of a bond.

Premium bond A bond selling at a dollar price above par and whose yield, therefore, is less than the coupon rate.

Prerefunded bonds A municipality may sell a second bond issue placing the proceeds of the issue in an escrow account from which the first issue's principal and interest will be repaid when due.

Primary market An over-the-counter market in which new bond issues are offered to investors for the first time.

Principal The face value of a bond, exclusive of interest.

Principal-only bond See PO STRIP.

Private activity bond (PAB) A bond whose proceeds benefit a nonpublic issuer, such as an airport revenue bond, where even though the facility may be owned by a public, nonprofit authority, airlines or concessionaires receive a benefit from the bonds. Depending on the purpose of the bonds, interest on private activity bonds may be subject to the alternative minimum tax (AMT) or federal income tax.

Prospectus A legal document offering securities (or mutual fund shares) for sale, required by the Securities Act of 1933. It must explain the offer, including the terms, issuer, and objectives (if a mutual fund) or planned use of the money (if a security). It must also provide, as appropriate, historical financial statements and other information that could help an individual decide whether the investment is appropriate for him or her.

Put A put gives the investor the right, but not the obligation, to redeem a security on a specific date that is prior to maturity. A put is an attractive feature for investors as it offers protection against rising interest rates. A put is thus a form of insurance, for which investors are willing to pay a premium. That premium comes in the form of a lower interest rate.

Ratings Various alphabetical and numerical designations used by institutional investors, Wall Street underwriters, and commercial rating companies to give relative indications of bond and note creditworthiness. Standard & Poor's and Fitch Investors Service Inc. use the same system, starting with their highest rating of AAA, AA, A, BBB, BB, B, CCC, CC, C, and D for default. Moody's Investors Services uses Aaa, Aa, A, Baa, Ba, B, Caa, Ca, C, and D. The top four grades are considered investment-grade ratings.

Real estate investment trust (REIT) A corporation or trust that uses the pooled capital of many investors to purchase and manage income property (equity REIT) and mortgage loans (mortgage REIT). REITs are traded on major exchanges just like stocks.

Real returns Returns that reflect purchasing power as they are adjusted for the impact of inflation.

Redemption The process of retiring existing bonds at or prior to maturity. It also refers to redeeming shares in a mutual fund by selling the shares back to the sponsor.

Refunding bond The issuance of a new bond for the purpose of retiring an already outstanding bond issue.

Registered investment advisor A designation representing that a financial consultant's firm is registered with the appropriate national (SEC) or state regulators and that the RIA representatives for that firm have passed the required exams. RIA is not a professional designation.

Reinvestment risk The risk that future interest and principal payments when received will earn lower than current rates.

Revenue bond A municipal bond whose debt service is payable solely from the revenues derived from operating the facilities acquired or built with the proceeds of the bonds. See GENERAL OBLIGATION BOND.

SEC Securities and Exchange Commission.

Secured bond A bond backed by a form of collateral.

Secondary market The trading market for outstanding bonds and notes. This is an over-the-counter market; a free form negotiated method of buying and selling, usually conducted by telephone or a trading system such as Bloomberg's.

Securitization The process of aggregating similar instruments, such as loans or mortgages, into a negotiable security.

SEC yield A yield quotation for mutual funds, based on a calculation established by the SEC. The SEC yield is an annualized return based on the most recent thirty-day period. It divides the net investment income earned (after expenses) by the maximum offering price per share on the last day of the period. The SEC yield may be more or less than the fund has actually earned in the period. SEC yield will not necessarily predict future returns.

Serial bond A bond of an issue that features maturities every year, annually or semiannually over a period of years.

Sharpe ratio A measure of the return earned above the rate of return on riskless short-term U.S. Treasury bills relative to the risk taken, with risk being measured by the standard deviation of returns. Example: The average return earned on an asset was 10 percent. The average rate of one-month Treasury bills was 4 percent. The standard deviation was 20 percent. The Sharpe ratio would be equal to 10 percent minus 4 percent (6 percent) divided by 20 percent, or 0.3.

Sinking fund Money set aside on a periodic basis to retire term bonds at or prior to maturity.

Sinking fund schedule A schedule of payments required under the original revenue bond resolutions to be placed each year into a special fund, called the sinking fund, and to be used for retiring a specified portion of a bond issue prior to maturity.

Skewness A measure of the asymmetry of a distribution. Negative skewness occurs when the values to the left of (less than) the mean are fewer but *farther* from the mean than are values to the right of the mean. For example: the return series of –30 percent, 5 percent, 10 percent, and 15 percent has a mean of 0 percent. There is only one return less than zero percent, and three higher; but the one that is negative is much further from zero than the positive ones. Positive skewness occurs when the values to the right of (more than) the mean are fewer but *farther* from the mean than are values to the left of the mean.

Spread The difference between the price a dealer is willing to pay for a bond (the bid) and the price a dealer is willing to sell a bond (the offer).

Stable-value fund Fixed-income investment vehicles offered through defined contribution savings plans and IRAs. The assets in stable-value funds are generally very high quality bonds and insurance contracts, purchased directly from banks and insurance companies, that guarantee to maintain the value of the principal and all accumulated interest (see chapter 6).

Standard deviation A measure of volatility or risk. For example, given a portfolio with a 12 percent annualized return and an 11 percent standard deviation, an investor can expect that in thirteen out of twenty annual periods (about two-thirds of the time) the return on that portfolio will fall within one standard deviation, or between 1 percent (12 percent − 11 percent) and 23 percent (12 percent + 11 percent). The remaining one-third of the time an investor should expect that the annual return will fall outside the 1 percent to 23 percent range. Two standard deviations (11 percent×2) would account for 95 percent (19 out of 20) of the periods. The range of expected returns would be between − 10 percent (12 percent − 22 percent) and 34 percent (12 percent + 22 percent). The greater the standard deviation, the greater the volatility of a portfolio. Standard deviation can be measured for varying time periods, e.g., you can have a monthly standard deviation or an annualized standard deviation.

STRIPS A bond, usually issued by the U.S. Treasury, whose two components, interest and repayment of principal, are separated and sold individually as zero-coupon bonds. STRIPS is an acronym for Separate Trading of Registered Interest and Principal Securities.

Subordinated debt A debt that ranks below another liability in order of priority for payment of interest or principal.

Swap The exchange of one bond for another. Generally, the act of selling a bond to establish an income tax loss and replacing the bond with a new security of comparable credit quality and maturity.

Syndicate A group of investment banking firms that agree to underwrite or purchase a new bond issue and reoffer it for sale to the general public.

Systematic risk Risk that cannot be diversified away. The market must reward investors for taking systematic risk or they would not take it. That reward is in the form of a risk premium, a higher *expected* return than could be earned by investing in a less risky instrument.

Taxable equivalent yield (TEY) The yield an investor would have to obtain on a taxable corporate or U.S. government bond to match the after-tax yield on a municipal bond.

Taxable municipal bond A municipal bond whose interest is not exempt from federal income taxation.

Tax-exempt bond A bond exempt from federal, state, and local taxes (at least if the owner is a resident of the issuer's state). This tax exemption results from the theory of reciprocal immunity: States do not tax the interest on instruments of the federal government and the federal government does not tax interest of securities of state and local governments.

Technical default A default under the terms of the bond indenture, other than nonpayment of interest or principal. Examples of technical default are failure to maintain required reserves or to maintain sufficient coverage ratios. Generally bondholders may, but are not required to, force the issuer to pay off the loan immediately if the bond is in technical default.

Term-to-maturity The number of years left until the maturity date of a bond.

Territorial bond A bond issued by Puerto Rico, the Virgin Islands, or Guam. Interest on this debt is exempt from federal, state, and local income taxes because of congressional action that provides these territories with such benefits.

Three-factor model Differences in the performance between diversified equity portfolios are best explained by the amount of exposure to the risk of the overall stock market, company size (market capitalization), and price (book-to-market [BtM] ratio) characteristics. Taken together, research has shown that the three factors on average explain more than 96 percent of the variation in performance of diversified stock portfolios.

TIPS Treasury inflation-protected security. A bond that receives a fixed stated rate of return, but also increases its principal according to the changes in the Consumer Price Index. Its fixed-interest payment is calculated on the inflated principal, which is eventually repaid at maturity.

Tranche One of a set of classes or risk maturities that comprise a multiple-class security such as a collateralized mortgage obligation.

Transparency The extent to which pricing information for a security is readily available to the general public.

Treasuries Obligations that carry the full faith and credit of the U.S. government.

Treasury bills Treasury instruments with a maturity of up to one year. Bills are issued at a discount to par. The interest is paid in the form of the price rising toward par until maturity.

Treasury bonds Treasury instruments whose maturity is beyond ten years.

Treasury notes Treasury instruments whose maturity is beyond one year, but not greater than ten.

Two-factor fixed-income model Differences in returns of fixed-income portfolios are explained by the two risk factors of term and default (credit risk). The longer the term-to-maturity the greater the risk, and the lower the credit rating the greater the risk. The markets compensate investors for taking risk with higher expected returns. Note that individual security selection and market timing are not systematic risk factors and, therefore, should not be expected to add value.

Unsecured bond A bond that is backed solely by a good faith promise of the issuer.

Unsystematic risk Risk that can be diversified away. Because the risk can be diversified away, investors are not compensated for taking unsystematic risk.

Volatility The standard deviation of the change in value of a financial instrument with a specific time horizon. It is often used to quantify the risk of the instrument over that time period. Volatility is typically expressed in annualized terms.

VRDO Variable-rate demand obligations (see chapter 10).

Yield curve Graph depicting the relationship between yields and current term-to-maturity for securities with approximately the same default risk.

Yield-to-call (YTC) Return available to call date, taking into consideration the current value of the call premium, if any.

Yield-to-maturity (YTM) Return available taking into account the interest rate, length of time to maturity, and the current price.

Yield-to-worst (YTW) A return calculation that considers the yield-to-maturity and the yield-to-call for every possible call date. The call date with the lowest yield-to-call is the one with the yield-to-worst.

Zero-coupon bond A discount bond on which no current interest is paid. Instead, at maturity, the investor receives compounded interest at a specified rate. The difference between the discount price at purchase and the accreted value at maturity is not taxed as a capital gain but is considered interest.

Acknowledgments

No book is ever the work of one person or, in this case, two people. This book is no exception. We would like to thank the other principals at Buckingham Asset Management and BAM Advisor Services, Susan Shackelford-Davis, Paul Forman, Steve Funk, Bob Gellman, Ed Goldberg, Ken Katzif, Mont Levy, Vladimir Masek, Irv Rothenberg, Bert Schweizer III, and Stuart Zimmerman for their support and encouragement. We especially thank Vladimir for his valuable insights and editorial suggestions.

We also thank Wendy Cook, Jared Kizer, and especially Laura Latragna for their contributions. Laura contributed many ideas that we hope have made the book an interesting as well as educational one. In addition, we thank Shannon Beam and Harold Walton of the fixed-income team at Buckingham Asset Management for their help. Any errors are certainly our own.

We are also greatly appreciative of the invaluable advice and suggestions made by Jackie Rosen of United Missouri Bank, St. Louis, Missouri.

Sam Fleischman, our agent, made many valuable suggestions. We cannot imagine a better relationship between authors and agent.

Larry adds the following: I would like to especially thank the love of my life, my wife, Mona, for her tremendous support and understanding for the lost weekends and the many nights that I sat at the computer well into the early morning hours. She has always provided whatever support was needed, and then some. Walking through life with her has truly been a gracious experience.

Joe adds the following: I would especially like to thank my mother and best friend, who was always there for me, had my best interests in mind, and provided inspirational guidance throughout my life. She has my lifelong love and appreciation. In addition, every book needs at least one person who is going to like it unconditionally.

Index

Index

Index

prudent strategy for, 4–5, 67, 213–14
to reduce risk of equity portfolio, 72–73, 144, 161
in retirement, 206–7
risk and, 4, 9, 22–39, 66–84
shifting-maturity approach to, 73–77
short-term securities and, 103–20
TIPS strategy for. *See* TIPS
withdrawal stage of, 81–82, 206–7
fixed-income specialists, 196
Flow of Funds report, 42
forecasting
consensus, 64
of future yield curves, 73–77, 201
of interest rates, 64, 202, 213
of the market, your need to ignore, 212
401(k) and 403(b) plans, 114, 117, 120, 205
Franklin, Benjamin, 2
fraud, 39, 49
Freddie Mac (Federal Home Loan Mortgage), 99, 101, 121
MBS of, 155, 161, 164
French, Kenneth R., 66, 126
funds
active vs. passive, 61–65, 67, 150–51, 203–4, 214, 235, 244
agency risk of, 38–39
cost of, 5, 67, 80–81, 109, 119, 150
performance of, compared to the market, 61–65
See also mutual funds *and other specific types of funds*

GAN (grant anticipation note), 185
general money-market funds, 107
GICs (guaranteed investment contracts), 115–16, 118
Ginnie Mae (Government National Mortgage Association), 12, 50, 101, 155
MBS of, 155–59, 161, 164
Gonzales, Laurence, 133
GOs (general obligation bonds), 175–76
government bonds, 85–102, 191
corporate bonds compared to, 32–33
See also municipal bonds; Treasuries
government money-market funds, 107
GSEs (government-sponsored enterprises), 11–12, 99–102, 121, 191
guaranteed-interest funds. *See* stable-value investment vehicles

health care municipal bonds, 28, 176–77
hedge funds, 130
Henning, Fred, 57
high-yield bonds (junk bonds), 125–34
definition of, 79, 121, 242
as hybrid securities, 127

insurers that sold GICs financed by, 115
risk of, 134
skewness and kurtosis of, 130–32
and type of tax account, 132–33
volatility of, 79
Hirsch, Yale, 1
housing bonds, 28, 176–77
hybrid securities, 5, 213
high-yield bonds (junk bonds), 127
preferred stocks, 137

I bonds, 93–95
indentures, definition of, 10–11, 241
industrial development bonds, 28, 176
inflation
equities' slightly negative correlation with, 90
Federal Reserve fight against, 21
MBS and, 159
TIPS and, 89–93, 222–25
inflation risk, 35, 82
initial offerings, 41, 87, 168, 193
liquidity and, 38
insurance companies
long-term obligations of, 70
for municipal bonds, 178–80
interdealer market. *See* wholesale market
interest-income funds. *See* stable-value investment vehicles
interest rate risk (price risk), 23–25, 78
balancing reinvestment risk with, 198–202
diversification of, 202
international diversification and, 143–46
most of returns from, 33, 191
symmetric and asymmetric, 135–36, 158, 160
TIPS and, 90–91
interest rates
avoidance of guessing about, 5, 202, 213
bond prices related to rise or fall of, 135, 157
forecasting of, by fund managers, 64
MBS and, 157–59
term structure of, 20
international fixed-term assets, 72–73, 142–53
CDs, 112
investment advisors. *See* RIA; separate account managers
investment banks, 41
investment-grade bonds, 26–28, 121–22, 242
investment policy statement (IPS). *See* IPS
IOs (interest-only bonds), 8
IPS (investment policy statement), 207–11, 213–14
IRAs (individual retirement accounts), 114, 117, 205–6

James, Bill, 65
Jensen, Michael C., 59–60

257

Index

Index

Index